One in the Spirit

Meditation Course for Recovering Couples

John Leadem, MSW
Elaine Leadem, MSW

One in the Spirit
Meditation Course for Recovering Couples
Copyright © 2010
John & Elaine Leadem

Library of Congress Control Number: 2010902111
ISBN: 978-0-615-28392-0
First printing: April 2010-400 copies

FOR INFORMATION CONTACT:
John Leadem
668 Commons Way
Building I
Toms River, NJ 08755
732-797-1444

Please visit our website at
www.leademcounseling.com.
Online ordering is available for this and other products as well.

Printed in the USA
By Morris Publishing®
3212 East Highway 30
Kearney, NE 68847
800-650-7888

Table of Contents

Welcome

Our union as husband and wife began on July 3, 1976. Our individual recovery efforts brought us together in the 12 Step rooms that each of us had previously claimed as our new homes. The steps and traditions were going to serve as the wise and caring *parents* that we both longed for and the fellowships that embraced us would be our *extended family members*. The recovery journey that began for John in 1971 and Elaine in 1975, while uninterrupted, has been anything but smooth. We were immature and traumatized *children* with a great deal to learn about ourselves and eventually about sharing our recovery with each other. The injuries we had endured and those we caused others and our marriage were the focus of many shared recovery moments that developed during our morning meditations. We intellectually understood that *hurt people hurt people* and came to experience at both emotional and spiritual levels the hopeful reality that *hurt people* could help one another heal if they were both *IN*. We each came into recovery seeking healing from our substance related addictions in both the roles of addict and children of alcoholic parents. We remained open to addressing other addictive illnesses that surfaced during the course of our early union and have known the warm reception as *beginners* at a variety of 12 Step fellowships.

The way to experience being "in love" is by making a decision to be "IN".

Our professional lives developed along intersecting paths that led us into a variety of disciplines and modalities that we would always infuse with the spiritual values that our surrogate *parents* and *extended family members* raised us to use as grounding rods. Our special affinity for recovering couples first inspired us to create and deliver our *Shared Program of Recovery©* model to couples in therapeutic retreat settings as well as conjoint insight oriented therapy. Now our belief in the healing power of a recovering coupleship brings you *One in the Spirit: A Meditation Course for Recovering Couples.* This course highlights the lessons we have learned in the recovery we have shared for the past thirty-three years in the hope that it will help you to be *IN*.

We are "IN" with you,

John & Elaine

Introduction

One in the Spirit is a meditative course in spiritual and emotional intimacy written for couples involved in 12 Step fellowships. When the honeymoon of early recovery fades, most of us become keenly aware that there is a great deal more to do after taking a 1st Step.[i] The identification of our powerlessness and unmanageability is the beginning of a process that creates the depth of personal change that allows us to participate fully in a love relationship.

This meditation course can be used as a resource for daily prayer and meditation, or as a reference for developing strategies to clarify and resolve conflict in a relationship. In spite of the frequent references to God, this meditation course is meant for people of all spiritual affiliations – religious, a-religious, agnostic, and atheist. Please understand the use of God to suggest the God of your understanding or your Higher Power. Likewise, the daily prayer is meant to help with spiritual grounding. A meditative scene or fond memory can be just as helpful.

Using Daily Meditations

The daily meditations can be used privately or with your partner. It is our suggestion that each of you first read the daily meditation privately and reflect upon its meaning in your own life. If you plan on working on the meditations alone, it is wise to share your insights with members of your support group. If you chose to work on the meditations with a partner, we encourage you to keep your sharing focused on your own experience, strength, and hope. Don't ask for advice because you may get it and don't give advice because your partner may take it.

Meditation Format

Each week will be devoted to a theme about relationship building that is broken down into five parts that will be introduced on a daily basis, Monday through Friday. Each daily meditation will address some aspect of the way the theme for the week can have an impact on the relationship. Each meditation will contain the following three key sections:

Challenge

The first section will briefly describe the challenges that we face in a romantic partnership. The challenge section is not intended to be a comprehensive review of the problem area or all of its common manifestations. It may introduce material that is unfamiliar to one or both of you or issues that you have not yet addressed in your individual or shared recovery. If the challenges for the day or the theme for the week generates emotional distress, make sure you take counsel with your support system, therapist, or spiritual advisor. Do not hesitate to skip themes that you find too distressing.

Reflection

This section suggests an alternate perspective on the problem addressed in the Challenge. The text is limited in scope and designed to aid the reader in self-examination. If you are interested in a more personal explanation of methods for responding to the challenge of your romantic relations, you can visit our library on our website at www.leademcounseling.com for expanded articles in themed areas of interest or concern.

Prayer

The meditation concludes with a prayer focus for the day that would be heightened if offered to your God with your partner. If the tool of prayer is not productive or a good fit for your spiritual plan for living then substitute it with a personally guided imagery that expands on the *reflection* or take a moment to listen to comforting music or establish a positive reflection on some aspect of your gratitude list.

The Weekend Workshop

The theme for the week will culminate in a Weekend Workshop that will be introduced on the sixth day of the theme. It is intended to be used by couples; however, you may work independently. If you are working alone, please share your concerns and insights with members of your support group. The guidelines for the workshop will offer activities to further explore the daily meditation themes and issues highlighted during the week. Exercises are offered with a focus on personal growth and relationship building. The amount of your sharing with your partner should be based on the relationship's emotional health and your personal spiritual fitness.

Starting the Day

Half Empty/Half Full

Challenge:

The challenges involved in nurturing a committed relationship can appear at times to be overwhelming. When we are overloaded it is easy to develop a distorted perception of our relationship. When we are too hungry, angry, lonely, or tired, it can seem like our partner is not measuring up. If our day begins with the view of life as a glass that is half empty, conflicts are bound to develop with people we encounter during the day, especially with people we are intimate with. A day that begins with life as a glass half empty is apt to drive us for more of everything else. When we struggle with the concept of just how much is enough we are going to have unreasonable expectations of our partner.

Reflection:

When it appears that we are stuck with a half empty glass we are going to assume that those who are supposed to care for us are not doing their job. It is common to decide that our partner is to blame. We will hear ourselves thinking, "If only my partner would!" It is time for self-examination. No person can be the "problem" with my life. Nor can any one person be the "solution" to the problems of my life. A life or a relationship that is viewed as half empty is headed toward empty.

Prayer:

God, help me to see my glass, my life, and my relationship as a vessel to be filled, not emptied.

Starting the Day

Prayer

Challenge:

The demands of life can sometime make for a frightening start to a day. Even though most of us retire at night with an expectation for the coming day there can be much about the day that is unknown. Whether you awake with an expectation that the day will hold challenges or promise the unknown variables can generate anxiety and fear. We can easily slip into preoccupation with problems of the past rather than anticipation for the promise of the future because most of us tend to project negative outcomes rather than positive ones. There could be much about the day that is outside of our control but we do not need to face it alone. If you have identified that changes will need to be made in this day, stop and ask for the power along with the courage to change the things you can and accept those you cannot. We cannot control the future but we do not need to face it alone.

Reflection:

Each new day or chapter of our life brings the promise of change and growth. While change is not a choice, whether or not we grow in this day is. The strength available to a relationship that places itself in your Higher Power's hands through common prayer is like a wellspring. There will always be change because we are always moving either backwards or forwards. It is easier to move forward during challenging times if you take your partner's hand.

Prayer:

God, help me to see my partner as an extension of your love and your power that I might better do thy will.

Starting the Day

Meditation

Challenge:

We all find it difficult at times to quiet the noise in our head when we listen for our Higher Power's will for us. It is easy to drift during times of meditation and reflection. Our spirit may desire a calm start to the day, but there "never seems to be enough time." The maintenance of a time for prayer and meditation can seem, at times, to be a daunting task. The needs of our family and friends and the obligations related to work and chores can consume a great deal of our waking hours. Making a spiritual connection with the God of our understanding can seem self-indulgent given the TO DO list some of us wake up with. We have tried, to no avail, to force prayer and meditation into our hectic schedules. No matter how many times we professed a new resolution to make time for meditative reflection and prayer we found ourselves breaking the commitment.

Reflection:

In order to maintain a healthy prayer and meditation life we would need to adjust our priorities and fit our lives around our prayer and meditation times instead of the other way around. When the early thoughts of the day are focused on ways of being of service to our Higher Power and our fellows the day has far fewer potholes. Maintaining a union with our partner during meditation time will help us to remain focused. We will have an easier time remaining grounded during the day when the day begins with a physical connection to a loved one of similar commitment. Holding hands during reflection time opens up the channel clogged by the things of the world to the knowledge of our Higher Power's will for us.

Prayer:

God, show me how to be still so I can better know your will for me. When my partner and I are united in our desire to feel your presence, it will be so.

Starting the Day

Refreshers

Challenge:

It is common for us to lose sight of the commitment we made at the start of the day. A day can blitz by in a flash and the emotional connection we made with our partner at the start of the day can be lost before lunchtime. The lost connection can make it impossible for you to be of service to your partner.

Reflection:

Taking time out during the day to reflect on the morning bond that began with shared prayer and meditation or the sharing of a reading will reunite you with your partner. Keeping your partner close at heart during the day can serve as a great source of support and security.

Prayer:

God, help me to remember those people whose support confirms your love for me.

Starting the Day

Focus On Service

Challenge:

The demands of the day can make it difficult to hear our Higher Power's will for us as individuals, much less as a couple. It is easy to become protective of our time together and withdraw from the recovering community we have grown up in, in order to have alone time with our partner. We do not and should not sever our relationship with our respective fellowship. The task is to weave these aspects of our lives together.

Reflection:

It is difficult to share the precious little time we have together with others. However, our communion with other couples allows our Higher Power to use us to strengthen the bonds that others seek for their partnership. Look for opportunities to share the love and empathy that is developing in your romance with the other people in your life. When we spread "us" to others, we will greatly increase the support that our relationship has available to it. When we allow ourselves to be used in this way, our love is intensified.

Prayer:

God, show us how to be of service to you in the lives of other couples. Provide us the opportunities to show others how you have loved us.

Starting the Day

Weekend Workshop

We hope that you have enjoyed a peaceful and optimistic start to the day each and every day this week. The meditations offered this week were aimed at those measures that each of us have available to us to "start over" each and every day. We hope that you take time each day to examine your perspective on the situations and events of your life. We have learned that the maintenance of a view of life as a glass that is half empty is emotionally and spiritually exhausting. We have come to believe that people are not born with optimism; instead, it is developed along with spiritual maturity, faith, and broadened perceptions.

John & Elaine

My Gifts to the Partnership

Look back to the early days of your recovery and reflect on the picture that you had at the time of what you needed to be happy. In what ways has the list of needs changed? Has your perception of what constitutes happiness changed? Write down your thoughts and share them in prayer. The daily practice of sharing your gratitude with your Higher Power and your partner can strengthen your bonds and improve your outlook for the future.

Share one thing with your partner that you no longer need to be happy.

Being of Service to Your Partner

How Can I Serve Thee

Challenge:

Many of us struggle with what to do when a loved one is troubled in some way. Some of us believe that we need to mind our own business: it is not my place to say anything! Others interpret detachment to be a license to disregard the responsibility for loving another person. Still others would rush into every problem to "fix it," regardless of whether or not they have permission.

Reflection:

While it is true that you cannot control the physical, emotional, and spiritual health of your mate, you share a responsibility for being of service to them when you are spiritually fit. Few people will be as well equipped as you are to see the signs that your mate is struggling, but personal interest can hinder the very best insight. If your words are selfish or hurtful, you are only hindering progress. If you want to be helpful, you must first look inside yourself. What is your personal identification with the problem and how might your life experiences be affecting how you are sharing your concern? Is your concern for your partner's struggle made worse by your fear of how it will affect your security? The struggles of our partner greatly influence us and if it is not our business, then whose business is it?

Prayer:

God, I offer myself to you to be of service to you and my fellows. Help me to treat my loved ones with the same dignity and respect that I would offer to a suffering friend or stranger. Help me to learn the difference between being responsible to someone and being responsible for someone. Help me to see the obstacles in me that stand in the way of my service to my mate.

Being of Service to Your Partner

Being a Part of the Solution

Challenge:

All of us, at times, find it terribly difficult to empathize with the pain of a loved one without slipping into judgment, criticism, or frustrating efforts to fix our partner. We feel justified in our frustration and growing intolerance because our partner does not appear to be doing much to help them. Our efforts to help are often rebuffed and we generally decide it is "not our place to say anything."

Reflection:

It is easy to get resentful about your inability to contribute to your partner's recovery. In the past, many of your efforts to be helpful have fallen on a deaf ear. Your partner seems ready to accept input from a stranger before being willing to listen to what you have to say, but why? Oftentimes it is not the content of the material we are discussing that will be unsettling for our partner, but the way in which we are attempting to deliver the information. All too often our delivery is spoiled by the feelings associated with experiences in which we were hurt by our partner or others. We may not be initially aware of the presence of these resentments but they can be awakened in us when our partner gets defensive about what we are saying. If you want to be a part of the solution rather than contributing to the problem, you will need to examine and resolve past resentments about your partner's resistance to your help. A thorough processing of aspects of your 6th and 7th Step work that impact your relationship will usually be of immense value.

Prayer:

God, you know my heart and the issues that are still unresolved for me concerning my partner's problems. Help me to see through my thoughts, words, actions, and feelings what I need to address in myself into order to serve you through my relationship with my loved one.

Being of Service to Your Partner

Detachment vs. Responsibility

Challenge:

Learning how to detach from the problems and mood swings of a partner is a difficult task for many of us. Detachment is understood to involve a "disconnection" from the lives of our mates when they are troubled. How do I serve my partner in a way that shows my love for them rather than my responsibility for them?

Reflection:

It is easy to say that the emotional and spiritual well-being of your partner is not your problem. However, such a position of complete separation will rob your partner of needed love, support, and insight. Instead of totally disconnecting, you may be able to help at one of these crucial times with gentle and rigorous honesty. This does not suggest that it is acceptable for your partner to blame you for the qualities of his/her life or that you are responsible for making it better. We are encouraging your involvement in the solution, not asking you to fix the problem. You can be helpful by sharing your concerns, experience, strength, and hope without trying to control the outcome. A healthy balance can be obtained that lies somewhere in between being totally disconnected and being the "fixer." Because we have found that we are either a part of the problem or a part of the solution in relationships, we have learned to be responsible first to our Higher Power and then to each other. Do not post the blame. Do not accept the blame. Moreover, do not ignore your responsibility. Detachment is not a break of contact or a separation.

Prayer:

God, I pray that you show me a way to be of service to you in the life of my partner who is suffering. Remove from me the self-serving fear and desire for self-protection that stands in the way of my usefulness to my partner. Show me how to love him/her the way you do. Help me to see my own identification with their suffering and trust that you are there for him/her when he/she is ready. Help me to avoid being an obstacle in his/her journey to your wisdom and understanding.

Being of Service to Your Partner

How Can I Allow Those I Love to Hurt

Challenge:

It has been said, "pain is the touchstone of all spiritual progress." Yet when we see a partner in physical, emotional, or spiritual pain, we often look desperately to find ways to "fix it." If it is true that we grow when we hurt, why am I so quick to intervene in the life of a loved one? What can I do to allow them their own journey through the pain?

Reflection:

When you choose not to hide your concerns from your partner, you have made a loving decision. Your partner needs your insights as much as you need theirs. Be cautious, however, because your partner needs your experience, strength, and hope, and not your advice. If you have your partner's permission to relate your personal experience and you deliver your concerns in a loving and nonjudgmental way, you can be of great service. If you barge in and impose your solution on your partner, he/she is likely to see you as part of the problem and retaliate. The most loving part of your action will be your decision, once you have shared your concern, to leave your partner to process the input with the God of his/her understanding. He/she may seek the support of fellow sufferers or professionals.

Prayer:

God, show me the sober way to respond to the pains of the people I love. Show me how to use my experience, strength, and hope to support my partner without forcing my will on them. Help me to learn more about the ways in which pain is a touchstone for spiritual progress.

Being of Service to Your Partner

Pain in Our Relationship: A Touchstone of Our Progress

Challenge:

Many recovering relationships are riddled with pain from the devastation of alcoholism and other forms of obsessive dependencies. The presence of pain during the active days of our active disease is understandable. However, many of us fear that the pain we encounter as we try to mend the wounded relationship is an omen of failure. How do I continue to work on my relationship despite the fear I have of the pain we are experiencing?

Reflection:

Many newcomers to recovery are taught early on that "pain is the touchstone of all spiritual recovery" because it is hoped that they will understand that recovery is not going to be all sweetness and light. It is important to maintain gratitude for all that recovery has given you, but remember that change often requires pain. Pain is viewed by many members to be the stepping off point to spiritual progress. A closer look at the origin of the word "touchstone" may reveal more. A "touchstone" is meant to be a standard for measuring the quality of something. In the past, a hard black stone, such as jasper or basalt, was used to test the quality of gold or silver by comparing the streak left on the stone by one of these metals with that of a standard alloy. Thought of in this way, the "touchstone" of pain and the way we cope with it is a wonderful way of measuring the depth or quality of our spiritual lives together.

Prayer:

God, help me to see the pain in our relationship as an opportunity to bring you into the center of "us." Too often, we run at or from each other because we do not want to be hurt. We go to such efforts to avoid the pain of growing that we cause new injury. Show me how to measure the quality of our spiritual life by the way that we respond to the pain that we experience in our relationship.

Being of Service to Your Partner

Weekend Workshop

We hope you have enjoyed our review of this week's theme. The dictionary defines a "servant" as someone who is submissive and in debt to another or someone who works out of obligation or duty. Your service to your partner can be an integral part of your growing relationship with the God of your understanding because the 7th Step Prayer calls us to be of service to others. It reads: "My Creator, I am now willing that you should have all of me, good and bad. I pray that you now remove from me every single defect of character that stands in the way of my usefulness to you and my fellows. Grant me strength, as I go out from here, to do your bidding (Alcoholics Anonymous, p. 79).

We were both terrified with the idea of "two becoming one" in marriage. One of us, we feared, would be the weaker and the other the stronger. The practice of the 12 Steps in our marriage has helped us to serve each other without losing our individual identity. The following exercises are offered as a method for enhancing the quality of your relationship. Avoid asking for or giving advice, refuse what appears to be justified criticism, and treat each other with the utmost dignity and respect. Enjoy your relationship. It is your Higher Power's gift to you.

John & Elaine

My Gifts to the Partnership

It may prove to be very beneficial to stop before you enter into your mate's struggles and consider your own emotional reaction to the struggle. A review of your personal identification may reveal important information about your motives. Time spent journaling on these questions (which can later be shared with a member of your support group) might contribute a great deal to your relationship's health. Choose the questions that you can most identify with: have I done anything to contribute to my partner's suffering for which I need to make an amends? If so, consider addressing the defect of character that generated your objectionable behavior by examining it in the 4th through 7th Steps before making amends. Can I identify with my mate's problem and am I at peace with the identification?

When you have a good sense of all that is going on in you and have shared your discovery with another individual, you may choose to offer your mate input about their struggle: ask your partner's permission to give them input. Let your partner know about the concerns you have about offering them input. Do not present your view with certainty because it is only your perception. Share your information as a concern, not a criticism. Stay in the moment and avoid referring to past experiences. Share your identification with the struggle and let your partner know that he/she is not alone. Offer to pray with him/her or offer him/her up in solitary prayer. Consider going to a meeting together. Let him/her know what you could do for them which would free them up to devote their time and emotional energy to getting peace back into his/her recovery. Some examples might involve assuming chores, parenting responsibilities, or other obligations that are too much for him/her to handle right now. Remember, you can only carry the message.

Let the Slogans Guide You

But for the Grace Of God

Challenge:

You look at your partner and think to yourself: why doesn't he/she take better care of himself/herself? You are certain that your partner would be better off and be less stressed if only he/she would do as you have suggested. You have an idea of what steps your partner is avoiding and why he/she is neglecting to practice the principles of recovery in all of his/her affairs. He/she is stuck again! When will he/she work the program the way I do?

Reflection:

It is easy to focus on the wrongs of others. We can see the weaknesses in our partner's program with true clarity. We can judge, nudge, and begrudge, but can we empathize? When someone in your home group is stuck again, do you look upon them with suspicion? It seems much easier to invoke the slogan, "But For The Grace of God" when the troubled person is someone other than your partner. When used in reference to a fellow sufferer the slogan is remembered with love, understanding, and genuine compassion. The empathy we feel for his/her struggle is matched only by the gratitude we feel for being spared the same malady or relieved that we have been set free from it. This freedom is a gift that is an aspect of the grace of God. If it is a gift arising from his grace, why do we take so much credit for our position in life when we are judging our partner? You have worked hard at your program and deserve to be proud of your commitment but the fact that you have succeeded in your recovery is a gift.

Prayer:

God, help me to better understand the ways in which your grace is a gift. Help me show others the gifts that I have been given. Give me the humility to always give you the credit. When my partner is hurting, let me remember that it is only by your grace that I am not.

Let the Slogans Guide You

Keep It Simple

Challenge:

The effect of alcoholism or other obsessive dependencies on a romantic partnership can be devastating. We assume that the wreckage of the past is going to take time to clear away. Most of us imagine that the relationship will survive; however, we understand that there are no guarantees. The fear of a failed relationship after entering recovery can be overwhelming. This fear may cause you to delve too deeply in the wreckage of the past at a time when the relationship is too fragile for this exploration. Far too many "why" questions are asked of our partners and ourselves. When asked why a particular event happened in the past, the answer, if it is honest, is far more than we are ready to handle. How does a recovering couple continue to work on the relationship without applying too much pressure?

Reflection:

The early months, perhaps years, of the relationship in recovery should focus on the simplicity of relationship building. It is generally understood that it is too soon to explore each other's past motivations or lingering defects of character, but the principles of recovery can be applied on the very first day. Consider these simple principles: treat your partner with dignity and respect, do not ask for or give advice, and pray together.

Prayer:

God, help me to move slowly. You know the fear that hampers my faith. Let me see where my partner and I are experiencing changes. Help me to treat my partner as I would a newcomer in my home group. Show me how to be a student of my partner's recovery experiences. Let me learn to share my own insights without attempting to manipulate my partner. Enable our relationship to show others that recovery, as a couple, is possible. Give us the courage to come to you in joint prayer.

Let the Slogans Guide You

Let Go and Let God

Challenge:

How do you go about the responsibility of being of service to your partner while practicing letting go of control? There would seem to be a bit of contradiction in the two. What do I address with my partner and what do I ignore? If we borrow some of the wisdom of the Serenity Prayer we will see that we can only really change ourselves. Our service to our partner cannot be designed to change them.

Reflection:

Encouraging you to "Let Go and Let God" does not mean that you should ignore the problems that you see. Bring your concerns forward to your partner if you have his/her permission to do so. It is the consequences of bringing out your concerns over which you have no control. We are encouraging you to let go of the outcome. Your partner may refuse to receive your input – LET GO. Your partner may not act in a way that you feel is appropriate or timely – LET GO. You may not feel the personal relief that you sought when you decided to reach out to your partner – LET GO. Your partner may hear from a friend the same input you delivered several weeks ago and find the friend's input most valuable – LET GO. Once you have served up your concerns – LET GOD love your partner in ways that you are not capable.

Prayer:

God, help me to remember you when I am trying to be of service to my partner. So often I get confused and frustrated. I have trouble knowing how much is enough. I am afraid of the outcome of sharing my concern and forget that my partner has a Higher Power as well. Help me to see your power in all that I do. Grant me the humility to accept that you will take care of my partner's needs.

Let the Slogans Guide You

One Day at a Time

Challenge:

Many of us have been deeply hurt in our romantic relationships. Sometimes our partners hurt us; other times we have been shamed by our behavior toward them. Learning to live "One Day At A Time" in a romantic relationship can be very difficult. Past wounds seem to be reopened with each new harm we experience or cause.

Reflection:

It can be difficult to stay in the moment when your partner is behaving in a way that you find hurtful. The normal tendency is to quickly remember all the times in the past when your partner has caused you pain. Painful memories awaken so quickly that it is also common to unknowingly re-experience feelings linked with the hurts associated with other partners. The recollection of past hurts will cause the present situation to appear much worse than it actually is. Likewise, when we are feeling ashamed of the way that we have injured a loved one, we are likely to awaken the feelings from past experiences as well. It is difficult to examine one's wrong in a fair light when we have one foot in the future fearing what will come and one foot in the past dreading repetition. Stay in the day and live the relationship one day at a time.

Prayer:

God, you understand that my feelings do not know what time it is. Help me to keep perspective. If today is painful, help me to stay with today instead of drifting into the past where there is no hope. If today I have caused pain, help me to stay in the day so I can see where I can change for the future. I am not who I was and I am not yet who I would like to be. Help me relate to my partner with loving, romantic awe.

Let the Slogans Guide You

Let It Begin with Me

Challenge:

How often do I look at my partner and think, "Gosh, I wish the nagging would stop!" or "I am sick of the mood swings and the outbursts!" At these times it seems so obvious that my partner is the broken one. We can hear our sponsor's voices saying, "What about the spiritual axiom that says whenever we are disturbed, no matter what the cause, there is something wrong with us?" But we are quick to rebuff the voice by establishing the certainty that we are "somewhat at fault, but our partner is more to blame!" These are difficult times in a relationship because it is much easier to run than work. Work needs to be done and we wish our partner would "get to it!" By the grace of God we hear the slogan "Let It Begin With Me."

Reflection:

The slogan is a gentle but affirming reminder that I need to look at myself first. "But why?" we ask. Many of us have come to understand that we see the defects in others that we can most identify with. The way our defect manifests itself may be somewhat different from our partner's, but we are likely to have similar or compatible defects. This is where the difficulty comes in. When defects are compatible like "bullying" and "being the victim," there will be many problems. This cycle needs to stop and the process needs to begin with you.

Prayer:

God, I am ready to act when I am chosen. Too much time has been spent arguing about who should go first and whose turn it is to make amends. Help me to step up to the task of being a loving person. Help me to be remembered as someone who loved fully.

Let the Slogans Guide You

We hope you have enjoyed our review of this week's theme. The slogans we chose to focus your attention on have been particularly helpful to us over the years. They are simple ways to get back on track when self-will has temporarily derailed us. We once used them like weapons when we would hurl them at each other in anger. Screaming at the other person to live "ONE DAY AT A TIME" never really seemed very spiritual. Today we use them to encourage each other and to motivate ourselves. We hope you will appreciate their simple wisdom. Our interpretation of their meaning may not be yours. They speak to each of us differently.

John & Elaine

My Gifts to the Partnership

In *Alcoholics Anonymous* (1953), the author introduces the fellowship's early slogans as "mottos" in the Ninth Chapter titled "The Family Afterward." The motto's read: "First Things First," "Live and Let Live," and "Easy Does It." Before introducing the slogans, the author describes a brief account of a member's relapse that begins with a marital conflict about the behaviors of one partner that the other partner wished to change. Although controlling behavior on the part of a mate is clearly not a justification for relapse, the story has merit. Neither partner in the relationship appears to have been sensitive to the pain of the other. One was thought to be in the wrong while the other believed himself to be in the right. Consider the slogans that were introduced during the daily meditations to be benchmarks for your acceptance and tolerance of your partner. Your efforts to use them in your relationship will encourage your partner and comfort you. But how do we monitor their presence in our lives? Take each slogan and answer the following questions with regard to each one: What am I thinking when the slogan is guiding me? What am I feeling when the slogan is guiding me? How am I behaving when the slogan is guiding me? What am I saying when the slogan is guiding me?

It might appear quite risky to expose yourself emotionally to your partner, but consider sharing the profile that develops when you answer each of the questions above. Avoid offering your partner any input and avoid soliciting input from your partner. This exercise is designed to build trust through self-exposure, not a discussion. It should not become an interrogation and is not intended to facilitate a 5th Step quality report. You are trying to help your partner get to know you. Your efforts to "squeal" on yourself will be rewarded.

Improving Communication

Please Hear What I Am Not Saying

Challenge:

We want our partner to know what we feel and what we need by reading our minds. It seems so easy to communicate with other people in recovery. Why is it that my attempts to talk genuinely with my partner often end in disaster? Perhaps my partner doesn't really care about me or us. I know relationships take a great deal of work, but every time we try to address our problems we end up in a fight!

Reflection:

It seems to be much easier to understand and nurture a stranger than to do the same for a partner, but why? We look at our relationships in recovery and proclaim that intimacy and trust are valuable goals to work for in a relationship. In our partnership, we feel we should be able to communicate as intimately as we do with our fellow group members. While in our meetings, our common trials are a source of strength and unity. The opposite is often true in our romantic partnerships where our common suffering is a source of anger and tension. The topics of discussion in early recovery tend to focus on the situations that have been the most painful. It is difficult, if not impossible, to begin to heal a relationship when the mere introduction of an uncomfortable topic generates pain and defensiveness. Often times we test our partner's love for us by whether or not they know what we want or need. The idea that the level of communication we practice will determine the breadth and depth of a relationship rings true here. If you want more than shared loneliness, stop testing your partner and begin revealing yourself.

Prayer:

God, help me to move slowly and purposefully through the learning that lies ahead. I know there will be many who will encourage me to accept less than you want for me in my partnership. Help me to grow where I am. Help me to have patience and willingness to work with my partner.

Improving Communication

But What More Do You Want to Know

Challenge:

For many of us, the level of sharing at a discussion meeting or during a speaking commitment is little more than a relating of facts. These are important facts to share as newcomers, but they have little to say about the emotional impact that our story has had on us or those we love. Most of us report feeling more than a little uncomfortable telling our story at a meeting attended by a romantic partner because our partners are likely to remember the emotional costs associated with the stories we are relating. The thought of honest sharing at a discussion meeting attended by a partner can be totally intimidating, but why? We can tell our stories to complete strangers, but fear rejection from those who love us. We complain that our communication with our partner is weak, but we often neglect to share even the simple facts of our story or the current emotional challenge to our sobriety.

Reflection:

It has been theorized that we fear the thought of telling another who we really are because they may not like the person we really are. In recovery, we have all known deep rejection and have also been the cause of lasting pain in others. We would like others to accept us the way we are, but are certain that they will not. As newcomers, many of us found acceptance we never thought was possible. They had learned what we would come to understand with time – we would know ourselves better when we invested ourselves in the lives of others. Have you invested yourself in the life of your partner? Does your partner know the facts about your disease's progression or you about theirs? Does your relationship have the benefit of regular input about what each of you are learning about yourself? Talk with your partner about the past and current life experiences that have shaped your personality. Be a student of your partner's past.

Prayer:

God, help me to begin the process of revealing myself to my partner. Show me how to share without expectation.

Improving Communication

I Know What You Believe, but I Do Not Know Who You Are

Challenge:

Amidst the defects of character that we have acquired, we have learned to play a myriad of games to prevent others from really getting to know the "real us." The games that we expect will keep us from getting hurt in our relationships with others really prevent us from developing the type of communication that leads to real intimacy and lasting romance. As couples move from superficial conversation to a deeper level of disclosure, the dialogue may begin to include thoughts, ideas, judgments and beliefs. It can be terribly frightening to risk revealing who we are. If I desire the self-knowledge needed to be intimate with another, I will need to be willing to share who I am without being blocked by the fears that haunt many of us. Am I ready to move forward with my partner?

Reflection:

It can be so frightening to tell my partner about myself that I wait for the moment when he/she begins to show disinterest so I can use it as an excuse to run. My partner may be distracted, but it may be because of fatigue or the problems of the day. The message in my head, however, is "my partner doesn't care about what I have to say and this is not worth it." What I am really saying is, "My feelings are hurt. I feel threatened because my partner's behavior seems to be a rejection. I have been here before. I do not like it." This can be a real time of reckoning. How many times when faced with perceived rejection have you begun an argument with your partner as a way of retaliating? This is an example of one of the ways we make decisions in fear. We are giving in to our old patterns of behavior and will be resentful when we end up with the same unproductive results. When you begin to reveal yourself to your partner, you are allowed to be frightened. When we settle for chitchat rather than revealing ourselves to our partner, we are settling for less than our Higher Power is offering.

Prayer:

God, you know the fear that I have of being hurt. Help me to trust in your care of me.

Improving Communication

But What Happens if You Do Not Like Me When You Find Out the Truth

Challenge:

All of us have had moments in a romance when we wished that we could retract what we said in anger or fear. We thought to ourselves, "I always make things worse when I say things in anger, but I can not seem to get to the truth otherwise." Communicating our feelings is vital to the growth of our relationship, but many of us appear to be so afraid of rejection that we wait until the emotion is boiling inside and the delivery is explosive. We fear that our partners will not tolerate such honesty from us. We choose to hide our feelings to avoid a conflict, but it comes anyway. This strategy causes the relationship to become more superficial. We make the mistake of exclusively sharing our true selves with our fellowship friends because we fear our romance cannot handle the truth. We aim to insulate our partner from our true feelings because we do not want to ruin a good thing. Eventually one of us explodes and the relationship is put at great risk!

Reflection:

Since the desire to produce emotional relief is the core trigger for relapse, the decision to share our true feelings will be central to our continued sobriety and the development of a healthy romance.

The way we feel is not a fact! Our feelings do not have to be justified. We do not need to wait until we are absolutely certain of the facts surrounding a situation before we share with those we love the feelings we are experiencing. Our partner does not need to fix what is wrong; he/she only needs to be willing to experience the sharing of the emotion with us.

Prayer:

God, help me to be who I am. Help me not to judge my emotions as either right or wrong. Help me to see my partner as a child of yours rather than a responsibility of mine.

Improving Communication

We Are One in the Spirit

Challenge:

To be an authentic person in my relationship and experience spiritual communication I must learn to be true to my partner and myself. In order to be true to myself, I will need to work toward being "one" me and not maintain different identities. To be true to my partner, I must give up my excuses for not being open (e.g. "this will be too hurtful to my partner" and "our relationship is not ready for such honesty"). This level of self-honesty will require that we aim toward perfection even though we understand that spiritual progress is all that is asked of us.

Reflection:

Our own emotional outbursts remind us that we either talk through our emotions or act them out – the choice is ours. Emotions build within us, gathering strength, regardless of what we do to dismiss them as wrong or inappropriate. If we remain emotionally disconnected in our relationship, our partnership will become brittle and fail to be a source of strength for either of us. We will begin to look and live like "married singles." The greatest gift we can give our partner is the gift of our true self. When we expose our true feelings to our mate and our mate returns the same, we are inviting a Higher Power into the center of our relationship. We also come to know our own goodness through the loving and accepting eyes of our partner. This is the path to becoming fully alive.

Prayer:

God, help me to become one in the spirit with my partner. Many will talk of separate programs and separate paths, but I have lived separate for far too long. I want to know the joy of spirit-filled romantic love that does not wrinkle with time.

Improving Communication

Weekend Workshop

This week's theme has caused us to reflect on the many hours spent (during the 33 years of married life) trying to understand how our Higher Power wanted us to love each other. Both of us grew up believing that the romance of a new relationship eventually had to give way to the mature companionship of a comfortable partnership. Neither of us expected to stay married under those restraints and we find ourselves grateful that we did not settle. The effort we put forward to learn to communicate at a feeling level has left us with a deep romantic love that grows richer and more exciting every day. Stick with it. You will not be disappointed.

John & Elaine

My Gifts to the Partnership

Begin a daily feeling journal that chronicles the feeling experiences that occur during the course of the week; look for patterns and triggers to the communication problems you are experiencing that you can share with your sponsor and your partner, if you choose. The material that you share with your partner should focus on your shortcomings and not those of your partner.

Examine an uncomfortable feeling experience that you had this week with your partner that left you confused about the motives behind his/her behavior. Imagine what life experiences he/she may have been exposed to that may explain the way he/she demonstrated the feeling he/she was having.

Explore the rules that you were exposed to as a child that may have influenced the way you deal with feelings today and share the memories with your partner. Examples: "Big Boys Do Not Cry" and "Girls Do Not Get Angry." Ask your partner to pray with you when you are disturbed about something that has occurred, provided it does not have to do with them.

Prayer of St. Francis-Part 1

Lord, Make Me a Channel of Thy Peace

Challenge:

When the peace of our relationship is threatened by outside forces, we are able to join against a common foe. When the peace of our relationship is threatened from the inside, we tend to blame or attack each other. For instance, when our relationship is facing the threats of externally caused economic insecurity (such as national economic slow downs), we find it possible to work through our individual fears and serve as a source of support for our partner. We may be afraid, but we have come to know that our Higher Power will see us through. However, when financial fears develop in reaction to the spending habits of our partner, we look to blame him or her for the condition of our checkbook and the way we are feeling. What will it take for us to be a channel of God's peace in the relationship when the threat to the relationship is coming from the inside?

Reflection:

In order to serve as a channel of peace to my partner, I will first need to accept the responsibility for the quality of my own life. Simply put, NO ONE CAN MAKE ME FEEL ANYTHING. I must take responsibility for how I think, what I feel, and how I behave. As long as I see change in others as the solution to my problem, peace will escape me. When I look to my partner to change what is wrong with me, I cannot be a channel of God's peace. I cannot have my partner as my Higher Power and I cannot be his/her Higher Power.

Prayer:

God, help me to be a channel of your peace. Sometimes I lack the presence of mind to know what is the next right thing to do in the relationship. Help me to see ways of drawing on your peace and use me to deliver it to those you would have me love, the way you love me.

Prayer of St. Francis-Part 1

Where There Is Hatred May I Bring Love

Challenge:

If I build the walls high enough, no one can hurt me! Most of us have been experienced construction engineers: we built emotional fortresses that were designed to keep out hurt, rejection, disappointment, and other forms of emotional pain. Many of us learned to build walls of steel and glass and to fashion mighty suits of armor during a time in our life when any form of relief from harm was welcomed. But did they ever really work? Perhaps for a time they did. We could disconnect emotionally from the painful reality of the moment by drifting off to a distant place. The walls did seem to work, but we found much later in life that the pain was recorded and we were only spared the suffering for a short time. The pain that has come from the hatred we buried has, over the years, cost so much more than the original pain inflicted by the hated event or person. Now, the walls seem to form even when they are not needed. Our archaic protection now hurts others as our sarcasm, cynicism, and negativity cuts at the spirit of those we love and slowly dismantles romantic relationships.

Reflection:

Many of us tend to hurt the one we love the most because our expectations are unreasonable. We expect that a romantic love should be pure and that our partner should never disappoint or hurt us. We tend to leave our partner a very small margin of error. Invariably, they do not measure up. How do we learn to love in spite of the hurt? We must decide to love because of the hurt that we have endured, not in spite of it! The walls must come down. The shields of indifference and negativity must be discarded. We must bring love or become like those from whom we tried to protect our own selves.

Prayer:

God, show me how to use the stones of the emotional fortress I have built to create grand entryways for others to feel welcomed. Help me to be clear about the source of my pain and hatred and not impose on my partner the responsibility for healing my past.

Prayer of St. Francis-Part 1

Where There Is Wrong, May I Bring the Spirit of Forgiveness

Challenge:

"You're wrong!" How many times have you been attacked with these words from a loved one? In response, how many times did you recoil in anger or hurl back an equally insensitive accusation? When we behave in this way within our relationships, we are making a decision to cut off communication and opportunities for personal growth. Our behavior looks and feels childlike because we are, in essence, throwing a tantrum. Children respond this way because they are not aware of alternatives. They have not had the opportunity to develop more appropriate ways to deal with their emotions and their reactions to others. As adults, we may also find that our choice of alternative behaviors is lacking so we resort to childlike attitudes and actions. Are you ready, in this moment, to seek out healthy ways to respond to your loved one that invites forgiveness and acceptance?

Reflection:

It may be helpful for you to recreate in your mind those moments when another has wronged you. This reflection may include past events in childhood or more recent times with your partner. Without judgment or criticism, meditate on how you are feeling and what images come to mind. Invite your Higher Power in to comfort you. In this state of consolation, ask for ways you may bring the spirit of forgiveness to your loved one. The wrong done to you may not be forgotten (at least at this time) but you can let go and seek the gift of forgiveness to flood your heart. It is not our job to right the wrongs of others. It is our opportunity to look for ways to share acceptance and understanding while remaining truthful with ourselves in this journey.

Prayer:

God, sometimes it is so difficult not to take the wrongs hurled upon me by my partner as personal injuries I must right. At these times, I am tempted to retaliate or to withdraw from my loved one rather than reach out to you for solace. I desire the willingness to offer acceptance and love to my partner. Show me how.

Prayer of St. Francis-Part 1

Where There Is Discord, May I Bring Harmony

Challenge:

Every relationship, whether it is romantic or social, will (from time to time) become embroiled. In social relationships we have learned to accept the shortcomings of those we care for and disregard the quirks in those relationships in which we had an investment. We can struggle more in our relationships with our children, but even with them we have learned to be more tolerant. However, when there is discord in our romantic relationship, we tend to have far greater expectations, a lower tolerance for imperfections, and reluctance to be the one to make the first move. "THIS TIME I WILL NOT APOLOGIZE FIRST!" We dig in our heels and the gap between us grows. When we do this, we are perpetuating the problem and drifting away from our Higher Power's grace and protection. We have been right for all the wrong reasons and wrong for all the right reasons.

Reflection:

Discord in a partnership should not be feared. The discord we experience is not prophecy that foretells the dissolution of our relationship. Discord is a wake up call. If we fail to respond, we might allow the relationship to flounder until there is too much pain to find a common ground. If we "answer the phone," but only with a willingness to address the problem after our partner accepts where he/she was wrong, we will eventually stop getting calls. Be willing to work toward harmony with your partner, just in case the call is from your Higher Power.

Prayer:

God, help me to keep my focus on your will for me rather than on proving myself right or my partner wrong. Show me how to help make sense out of discord through rational thought, empathetic feeling, encouraging words, and actions of service.

Prayer of St. Francis-Part 1

Where There Is Error, May I Bring Truth

Challenge:

There is great disagreement in our 12 Step fellowships about the path to follow when we have wronged another. Some will argue foolishly that the victim had it coming to them, but we know better. We have learned to avoid the temptation of unleashing our wrath. In an effort to avoid the discomfort of direct amends, there will be those who claim that "living amends" is more important than acknowledging the specific nature of our wrongs. Living amends are important because there can be no lasting change without them, but they cannot take the place of telling the truth, if that is possible. All too often, "living amends" become a way of hiding from the truth of our wrong. When living amends are the only form of amends used, it is likely that the wrongs will be repeated.

Reflection:

We all make mistakes. Whether my partner commits the wrong or I do, there can only be a lesson learned if we are willing to examine the defects of character that gave rise to the wrong. Many in the recovering community become disenchanted with the process of recovery when they continue to make the same mistakes. Yes, it is important that we remember that our goal is progress and not perfection, but it is much more important that we begin to understand the truth about our wrongful behavior. It is not enough to say, "I am sorry and I am going to live differently." If we do not develop an understanding of the function of our behavior and process that insight through the 6th and 7th Steps, we will begin to feel hopeless. The truth we seek can be found in a deeper understanding of what benefits we derive from the behavior that we keep repeating.

Prayer:

God, you know the sadness in my heart when I hurt a loved one. Help me to move beyond the childlike apologies that were intended to get me off the hook. Help me to see where I need to change so that my amends actually mend a wrong.

Prayer of St. Francis-Part 1

Weekend Workshop

The Prayer of St. Francis is both demanding and kind. St. Francis asked a great deal of himself and God's kindness provided St. Francis with self-honesty, insight, and a desire for personal growth. We have used the prayer as a soothing psalm and framework for measuring our spiritual progress. The prayer's components can be used to measure our relationship with our Higher Power. We hope you will adapt a way to monitor your spiritual progress. It will be that progress that provides the greatest insulation against relapse.

John & Elaine

My Gifts to the Partnership

Meditate on the opportunities you have to bring peace to those you love, especially your partner.

Share with your partner what ways they might be of service to you.

Avoid discussing changes that you would like your partner to make in them. Keep the focus on what changes you want to make for yourself and to improve the relationship.

The Promises-Part 1

We Are Going to Know a New Freedom and a New Happiness

Challenge:

Many couples have come to us in search of marriage counseling with the goal in mind to "save the relationship." They are full of doubt and fear and are somewhat suspect about the path we will lead them on in therapy; however, they are certain that they must do whatever is necessary to prevent the dissolution of the relationship. Most are surprised and somewhat disappointed to find that we do not have a plan for their relationship. In fact, we do not even know if the relationship warrants being saved. If you have waited until you are ready to throw the relationship at the mercy of a therapist, there has been a great deal of injury. Sometimes folks want to hear us say, "Yes, we agree that you two would be better off apart," but how would we know that? You must ask yourselves what you are looking for in a relationship, not whether or not a professional believes that your relationship can be fixed. Are you looking for permission to end it or are you looking for help to rebuild it?

Reflection:

It is important to remember that the "promises" are introduced at the end of the 9th Step in *Alcoholics Anonymous* (1953, p. 83). This would suggest that the freedom and happiness we are seeking would begin to materialize when we have straightened out the wreckage of the past. The soul searching and character building involved is hard work but the release we experience when we have faced the worst in us is liberating. If you are not experiencing that freedom and happiness in your relationship, perhaps it is because your relationship is outside the grace of your Higher Power. If you have not worked each of the nine Steps on your relationship, grace may elude you.

Prayer:

God, you have promised that I would know a new freedom and a new happiness. I see that promise being fulfilled in many areas of my life, but I long for the same joy in my romantic relationship. Give me the courage to apply the same nine steps that relieved me of the bondage of self to the romantic aspects of my life. Show me how to truly practice the principles of recovery in all of my affairs.

The Promises-Part 1

We Will Not Regret the Past, Nor Wish to Shut the Door on It

Challenge:

If you are over thirty, you may remember phrases like "do not cry over spilled milk" and "the past is the past...you should not live in the past." Those rules for coping with feelings were prominent when pop music discouraged "big boys" from crying and hit movies suggested "love meant never having to say you are sorry." There were so many rules for how we should feel or act that it is no wonder so many of us found ways to dull the pain of living.

Reflection:

While the journey down memory lane may be nostalgic, those rules for coping with and expressing our emotions will cause many problems in our recovering romantic relationships.

We agree that it is unhealthy to live in the past, but purposeful excursions into the past with people we trust can uncover valuable insights into the defects of character we struggle to let go of in the 6th Step. *Alcoholics Anonymous* (1953) suggests "we grow by our willingness to face and rectify errors and convert them into assets" (p. 124). Additionally, our past will be the source of infinite value to our partner or other couples if we are willing to share ourselves completely with others. "You are only as sober as your deepest, darkest secrets." We both recoiled from that admonition because we dreaded the thought that our partner would know the truth about our past. We had both experienced numerous romantic failures and suspected that our new relationship would suffer the same fate as the rest of them – disaster. We would start fresh and keep our past from our partner. If we choose to keep our past from our partner we will soon be amazed by the conflict it stirs.

Prayer:

God, help me develop the courage to be as vulnerable with my partner as I am with you. Reveal to me the truth about what motivates my actions and help me to use my past as a way of serving rather than manipulating others.

The Promises-Part 1

We Will Comprehend the Word Serenity and We Will Know Peace

Challenge:

All of us have known a great relief in our recovery. For some of us, the relief came with the burden of the obsession of getting high being taken from us. Others have known relief in the discovery that they are their own person and are no longer trapped on the emotional roller coaster of reacting to the other person's moods or behaviors. The serenity and peace we experienced at those times seemed like a miracle, but to our Higher Power it was just life as it should be. Why then, if serenity and peace are gifts from our Higher Power, are these emotional states so difficult to achieve in my romantic partnership?

Reflection:

In earlier meditations, we talked about the importance of being of service to your partner. You have known periods of serenity and felt true peace when your personal sacrifices resulted in gains for others. If you make physical, emotional, and spiritual sacrifices when the partnership appears to be in conflict, you will be richly rewarded with the peace and serenity that you seek.

Prayer:

God, I know that the service you request will bring difficult challenges, and I accept those challenges. Help me to remember that while the pain might be necessary, the misery is optional. Sometimes it seems like I enjoy the crisis, but you know that it is your peace that I seek. At times, the true path to your gifts of serenity and peace is hard to distinguish.

The Promises-Part 1

No Matter How Far Down the Scale We Have Gone, We Will See How Our Experience Can Benefit Others

Challenge:

Couples will often tell us that they have lost the magical feeling in their relationship. They want to reclaim the romantic charge they once shared during the early days of their recovery. Most of us will recall those early years as emotionally challenging and spiritually draining but full of tremendous personal and romantic rewards. In the beginning we made a lot of mistakes, but our relationship was thrilling and alive. Is it still thriving?

Reflection:

You are not falling out of love because it is not a place you leave or "fall" from. Love is a decision and the state of being in love is a way of describing the spiritual charge you get from your Higher Power's grace when you are both engaged in the process of becoming a partnership. If you have lost that feeling of being one in grace, consider looking for opportunities to be of service to other couples. *Alcoholics Anonymous* (1953, p.124) suggests that " … each family which has been relieved owes something to those who have not …" because " … showing others who suffer how we were given help is the very thing which makes life seem so worthwhile to us now." The past, the text suggests, may be the "greatest asset the family has and needs to be shared."

Prayer:

God, sometimes I can feel so alone in my partnership that the fear becomes overwhelming. Help me to open my relationship up to others so that fresh life can be let in and our experiences will have renewed purpose.

The Promises-Part 1

That Feeling of Uselessness and Self-Pity Will Disappear

Challenge:

Living with alcoholism and other forms of dependency can erode one's sense of security and feeling of competency. Emotional and spiritual needs routinely go unmet. As a result, a myriad of games are played in an attempt to manipulate others into fulfilling those unmet needs. Like most efforts to control other people, these games usually result in disappointment and emptiness, and the problem is really much bigger than learning to avoid manipulative games. We must come to an understanding that a romantic partner cannot make us feel useful or whole. The feelings of uselessness and self-pity are the result of believing that another person can make you feel whole. Your partner will undoubtedly miss the mark with such an expectation on his/her shoulders.

Reflection:

We often look outside ourselves for personal worth and fulfillment. The journey can be a long and painful one with very few moments of serenity and little in the way of personal fulfillment. We cannot find our fulfillment in another person. We cannot find purpose in life or lasting reward in a relationship that is viewed as a trophy to be won. Romantic conquests do not result in a sense of "self." These conquests instead produce short-term rewards and an insatiable appetite for the next competition. Likewise, when we place our personal worth and esteem in the hands of our partner, the acceptance or love we seek will remain unattainable.

Prayer:

God, help me to know your will for me. I long to be the best I can be rather than what others want me to be.

The Promises-Part 1

Weekend Workshop

It has been important for us to remember that the "promises" are placed in the recovery text Alcoholics Anonymous (1953, pp. 83-84) just before the description of the 10th Step. The implication, we believe, is obvious – we will be granted the gifts involved in the promises if we do the Step work prior to the 10th Step. We hope you will apply each of those nine steps to your relationship. We do not want you to miss out on the good stuff that follows.

John & Elaine

My Gifts to the Partnership

Examine the ways in which you have applied the first nine steps in your romantic relationship. The areas you find deficient need your attention.

Share with your partner the promises that you see coming true in his/her life.

Steps Toward the Fullness of Life

Accepting Oneself

Challenge:

This week's theme will examine the steps that are essential in developing a fulfilling life through the eyes of the recovering relationship. In the past, many of us did not feel as if we had really been living life and found ourselves looking for "real love" with little success. These pleas were most evident when we were lonely and longing for a partner to share our lives with, or were trapped in a relationship that appeared to be dying. Those of you who have struggled with romantic relationships as we have will understand that the desire to be loved by a partner can be a powerful force that can drive one blindly into a relationship that is apt to be lopsided and unfulfilling. Many dynamics in such a relationship create problems and threaten the relationship's health. One common problem we experienced was our tendency to switch sources for our self-esteem from being acceptable to our Higher Power and ourselves to sources we thought would be acceptable to our partner.

Reflection:

Many of us have entered into relationships because of the relationship's potential. We knew that there were problems, but we were sure that things would "work themselves out with time." Sometimes we thought to ourselves that we had enough romantic feeling to carry the relationship, but how wrong we were! Self-acceptance and a willingness to correct the flaws in our character had been the important features of our recovery prior to the relationship. What changed? If the relationship you are in survived active addiction, there is little doubt that each of you has suffered real injury to your self-esteem and sense of purpose in life. Avoid the trap of expecting that your personal worth can come from a romantic relationship. No relationship, no matter how healthy, can withstand that burden.

Prayer:

God, help me to avoid surrendering myself to my partnership. Help me to remember that I diminish my sense of self when I make my relationship my Higher Power.

Steps Toward the Fullness of Life

Being Oneself

Challenge:

"To thine own self be true." What a job that can be! During our active dependency we would, out of necessity, wear many masks. Some, we thought, were needed to protect us from hurt and rejection. Others, we theorized, would make other people happy and ultimately more accepting of us. Again, we were wrong! The masks or games we played to survive the painful realities of our active dependencies were indeed necessary evils. They served, at the time; to protect us from the painful consequences of the way we were living our lives. As we seasoned in our recovery, those games became traps and we lost sight of who we really were. They were once effective tools for coping with life. Now, they are rapacious creditors that will bankrupt our partnership.

Reflection:

For those of us who were exposed to homes impacted by dependency, the ability to read people and the environment for clues about how to behave and what to say was not a personality feature - it was a survival tool. Likewise, the fear and suspicion that develops in the lives of the victims living with obsessive dependency leaves them ever watchful of their surroundings either because they are trying to live in secret or because they are unaware of how they are being viewed by others. If we are going to be true to ourselves and honest in our partnership, there can be only one of us. The fullness of life will surely escape you if you try to please others by being who they want you to be. It is nurturing to make sacrifices for someone you love, but the sacrifice cannot be your very personhood. If you pretend to fit in or present yourself differently in different situations with different people, you will get lost.

Prayer:

God, help me to remain focused on the life you would have me live. Help me to define what I stand for and what I value. I understand that life is not a dress rehearsal and that I am not really practicing being a person. Help me to stay out in the open and near to you.

Steps Toward the Fullness of Life

Losing Self

Challenge:

During the past 33 years; we have had the honor of being asked to support others in numerous 5th Step experiences. Each time we begin the journey, we are excited about what we will learn about ourselves as a result of being willing to be of service to others. What a gift to have the opportunity to truly see the world through the eyes of another! There is great opportunity for growth in forgetting oneself in romance as a vital part of learning to live fully. In this, we try to listen with our hearts. The challenge is clear: can we learn to be truly empathic with those we would serve without judgment or criticism? Most of you have felt that acceptance during your personal sharing with a 5th Step confidant. Some of you have undoubtedly had the privilege of receiving a 5th Step that you accepted solemnly. Was the experience one of judgment or acceptance and emphatic listening? Is it different in your partnership? Do you receive what your partner shares with unconditional acceptance in the spiritual way that you received the innermost experiences of a newcomer to recovery?

Reflection:

It is our ego – our desire for control, manipulation, or possession that disconnects us from being able to forget ourselves when listening to our mate. The challenge of honoring our partner with this kind of loving reception is that it places us on equal footing. There is no "top dog" and no "underdog." Instead, the relationship is nourished by our ability and willingness to "become the other" for the brief moment we share in the revelation of the other's soul. It is one of the most unselfish gifts you have to offer, and one of the most joyous gifts you can receive from your partner.

Prayer:

God, your gifts are so plentiful. In this time of meditation, I surrender my ego and offer to lose myself in your name. I know this is possible as I am learning with grace and patience to forget myself in loving others. As I go forth in this day, I pray to see with your eyes, to hear with your ears, and to speak with your words.

Steps Toward the Fullness of Life

To Believe

Challenge:

During active addiction it is easy to get lost in the passion of our beliefs, especially if we were toxic or felt particularly justified in our obsessions. But for many of us, the principles or causes we desperately fought to defend changed with the wind. Many times our beliefs changed drastically when we entered a new romantic relationship. We wanted the "match" to be perfect, so we discarded certain beliefs in exchange for the approval of our partner. Or worse yet, we only pretended to believe what they believed and lived in constant disharmony with our inner self and the spirit in us. Now in recovery, we know that having a greater good and higher purpose for our existence is essential to the development of a full life. For most of us this is not a new concept. We have come to understand from our experience that a spiritual purpose beyond the limits of material and romantic security is crucial to continued sobriety.

Reflection:

The "promises" we introduced in previous meditations are describing, in part, how you can tell when you are in pursuit of the knowledge of your Higher Power's will for you. They also represent beliefs or values you may subscribe to. However you form your value system, it is important to know what you stand for. When the questions of right and wrong are clear, it is easy to choose the next right thing to do. Oftentimes the direction with regard to romance and true partnership is not clear. What do you want from a romance? What is the depth and breadth of your commitment? How is this romance being used to be of service? Have the courage to let other couples see what your relationship stands for. It may mean breaking some of the usual rules of social gathering, which tend to pair men with men and women with women. Demonstrate your love. Stay a couple.

Prayer:

God, so often I have drifted from the path and called for you while lost in the woods. Help me to journal in a way that shows me when I am getting lost.

Steps Toward the Fullness of Life

To Belong

Challenge:

Each of us has known the sense of belonging that comes with true partnership with our fellow sufferers in our respective 12 Step programs. Still, many of us have learned to live in isolation and self-sufficiency. We feared that the self-exposure we were experiencing in the fellowship would cause us to be hurt outside of the fellowship. We had spent a great deal of time learning how to be "apart" from others because we felt we had no choice. When we were confronted with the prospect of being "a part of" something, we were certain that we would not be accepted. We had an emotional awakening when we learned that we would be accepted not in spite of who we were but because of who we were. In romance it is common for us to forget all that we have learned about the spirituality of being "other centered" in the community of our fellowship. As adults, many of us regress to the behaviors of our adolescence when we isolate in a romance, even when we know that isolationism breeds relapse.

Reflection:

What do we belong to as a couple? Where do we serve others as a team? Each of us is concerned with being nurtured in our respective sobrieties, but what are we doing to nurture the relationship? Do the two of you have a place where your relationship would be missed? Expose your relationship to other couples and it (and they) will grow stronger.

Prayer:

God, help us to share freely what you have given us. Help us to be a beacon for those who find their relationship in trouble. The blessings you have provided in the form of patience and tolerance with each other will serve each of us as we go out from here to serve other couples as a team.

Steps Toward the Fullness of Life

Weekend Workshop

We hope you have enjoyed the meditations created for this week. It has been a real thrill to be sharing with you the treasures we have discovered in our marriage. You will find the treasure if you continue to believe that the Higher Power in your relationship loves the two of you.

John & Elaine

My Gifts to the Partnership

It has been our experience that our desired attitude changes have developed from the practice of prayer and service. Create a prayer that encompasses the changes that you desire for yourself. Commit the prayer to memory and recite it every day for a month.

Ask your partner to share his/her core values with you and the life experiences that helped to shape those values.

Seek permission to share your core values with your partner and the life experiences that helped to shape those values.

Avoid submitting any input, and keep any questions you have very simple.

Economic Security

Practicing These Principles in All of Our Affairs

Challenge:

We are promised in the recovery text *Alcoholics Anonymous* (1953) that the fear of economic insecurity will leave us. Many of us will quickly notice that this promise is slow to materialize. We will feel slighted as we watch those around us accumulate material signs of success and wonder "When will I get mine?" We are so tired of being broke or living from paycheck to paycheck. How long will we have to wait for the promised economic security to be granted to us?

Reflection:

Upon closer examination, usually at the insistence of our sponsor or spiritual advisor, we discover that we are not promised economic security. We are promised that the "fear" of economic insecurity will leave us. We are not promised wealth. We are not guaranteed a job, material success, or immunity from prosecution for financial mismanagement. What we are guaranteed is that we will be released from the gripping fear of 'not having enough'.

If we fail to practice these principles of recovery in all our affairs (including money management) we will know great economic insecurity.

Prayer:

God, help me to live the 12 Steps in all my affairs. Show me how to measure my worth in ways other than economic success. Help me to be grateful for the riches you have given me, for they are many. I know that when I measure my worth through possession I will be riveted with the fear of economic insecurity. Show me the way to a simple peace that has but one price tag – faith.

Economic Security

Living Within Our Financial and Emotional Means

Challenge:

Most of us have made purchases that our budget could not afford. Some of us learned that impulse spending to make ourselves feel better could carry a bigger price tag than we expected. Some of us are still recovering from those fantasy trips into the lifestyle of the "rich and famous." We have talked to many couples over the years that faced multiple bankruptcies in their recovery from "feel good" spending that got out of control. If we are practicing the principles of recovery in all of our affairs, how could this happen?

Reflection:

The reality for us, when we were overcome with credit card debt, was that we had not been practicing the Steps in all of our affairs. We spent money to purchase happiness, to impress other people, to fill a spiritual void created by some deprivation in our lives, or to ease the pain of "not having enough." The Steps that could work to clear away the wreckage of our pasts could certainly work on the drug-like spending that we were consumed with. The beginning of our return to sanity came with the recollection that our spending, like our drinking, had been but a symptom of our underlying spiritual malady. Purchases on credit were not our right - they were a trap. We needed to spend no more than we earned. This commitment to a budget based in reality, however painful at times, was similar to the establishment of abstinence from our first obsession.

Prayer:

God, show me how much is enough. Allow me to know the financial and emotional freedoms that come from living within a budget that reflects the reality of my life.

Economic Security

How Do We Measure Our Worth

Challenge:

It is not uncommon in our society to honor people who have substantial amounts of money regardless of the way they have accumulated their wealth. Wealthy individuals are seen as powerful, successful, and respectable – many of the attributes we seek for ourselves. It is easy to get lured into believing that our neighbors, co-workers, fellow 12 Step group members, family, etc. will view us in a more favorable light if we are financially secure. How many times have you defined your worth by the size of your checking account balance or the shine on your car?

Reflection:

One of the irrational expectations we have of ourselves is that we must be perfectly competent and successful in achieving material possessions or social status before we can think of ourselves as worthwhile. At first you may think, "I do not do that." In fact, you may even think this idea is ridiculous. However, some of us have accepted a position because we hoped the prestige would impress our spouse or co-worker. Others of us have stayed in a job we no longer found fulfilling because it offered economic security. Some of us have accepted money or gifts from family members when we knew the emotional cost was much higher than we wanted to pay. Maybe you have encouraged your partner to take a position or to stay in an existing job "for the family" while discounting his/her feelings of dissatisfaction with the job. In each of these situations, we allowed our fear of appearing incompetent or less than to make our decisions for us. This fear may take the form of desired approval, security, or power. In any case, the result is the same – spiritual bankruptcy. In making these choices, we had forgotten other ways of measuring our worth and money became our barometer of success.

Prayer:

God, my desire is to focus on the worthiness of the spirit world rather than the societal influences I face each day. Show me what I need.

Economic Security

What Have "Feel Goods" Cost Us

Challenge:

We define "feel goods" as those activities or objects that we acquire or pursue in order to generate sensations of wholeness, worthiness, respect, envy, love, acceptance, and the like. Most of us intellectually understand that we do not change from the outside in. At the same time, it is very difficult to give up the dazzle of a quick and seemingly harmless "feel good." Some seek "feel goods" through sexual flirtation while others prefer criticism of the shortcomings of others. Others purchase things that are impulsively obtained in an attempt to numb emotional pain or ease loneliness. These various actions and purchases will generally enlarge the hole the "feel good" was intended to fill.

Reflection:

Every "feel good" we pursue is more than we can afford because the relief that it generates disappears before we can really enjoy it. Also, more times than not, the "feel good" is replaced with guilt. So often "feel goods" are acquired in secret because we know they are dishonest. If we are discovered, we feel ashamed or become defensive and push away those that would cause us to undertake a closer examination of our motives. The shiny bauble that we desire is more valuable if we can deprive ourselves of it because the deprivation will allow us to understand what we were really looking for. Emotional wealth can be measured by the number of "feel goods" that we can leave untouched.

Prayer:

God, help me to look beyond the glistening luster of the gold chains that have so often been a source of emotional and spiritual bondage.

Economic Security

Celebrating the Success of Those Around Us

Challenge:

Many of us struggle with the tendency to measure our worth by comparing ourselves to others. We see friends living the lifestyle that we desire and we feel less than adequate. We compare our incomes to those of our colleagues and we feel less successful if their income is greater than ours. Our employer awards us a financial raise and we have spent it before we can really appreciate its value as a source of recognition for our hard work. We feel fulfilled in our relationship until we see others who appear to share more intimacy than we do. Measuring our worth in spiritual terms can be difficult, even with concerted effort. It is so easy to feel like we do not have enough and that we are ourselves are not enough.

Reflection:

When we are spiritually fit, we can enjoy the successes of others. If we can keep our focus on the spiritual gifts that we have been given, we will know great wealth. When we can celebrate the victories and accomplishments of others as if they were our very own, we will be true servants. But how do we reach that level of service? Look for opportunities to help others be successful.

Prayer:

God, help me to be grateful for the gifts that you give to others. Help me to see the benefit in helping others to succeed at the tasks that challenge them the most. I look to you for opportunities to bring the gifts of encouragement and unconditional love to those who struggle to be successful.

Economic Security

We hope you have enjoyed our brief journey into the realm of economic security. We have worked with many couples over the years that tell us that their relationship would have fewer problems if they were not so worried about the management of their finances. It is clearly one of the "hot spots" that couples in a committed relationship frequently argue about. Even so, the size of our checking account balance has never really been the problem. It has only been the symptom of a problem. Couples tend to fight about money, sex, and the way the other person is parenting. These, we assure you are, just symptoms of a larger problem. We have learned to listen to the signals we receive from these "hot spots" because they will always alert us to a problem that is usually spiritual and always tied to our defects of character.

John & Elaine

My Gifts to the Partnership

Identify what defects in your character (not your partner's) that contribute to your impulse spending. Impulse spending occurs whenever we have made a purchase that has not been saved for.

Write a letter to your partner describing what money had meant to you in your development and what your family's beliefs about money involved. If your partner is willing, read the letter without discussion of the contents or reaction.

When constructing the letter, avoid any references to your partner, ask no questions of your partner, and offer no input to your partner. This letter is solely intended for you to expose yourself to your partner so he/she can know you better.

The Faces We Wear-Part 1

Never Wrong

Challenge:

This week's theme will explore five faces that we use to keep our real selves hidden from detection and harm. These faces have developed in us over time and are intricately woven into the fabric of our personalities. These faces, like many of our defects of character, have been life preserving and, therefore, difficult to rid ourselves of. They cannot be taken from you, but the wearer is free to discard a face at will. He/she must be ready to take the risk toward a fuller life and a more intimate relationship. Those of us who are afraid of losing an argument or having our position and beliefs questioned play the "never wrong" strategy. When consumed with this mindset, we have been unable to hear the position offered by our partner. Our partner will be wrong no matter what the cost. And the cost in the early days of our relationship would always include the injuring of both of our spirits. When you are "never wrong," you can't really hear the feelings related to your past life experiences that are fueling the power-driven argument that you are determined to win. When you are "never wrong," you cannot hear what your partner is saying. You can only hear words, which you plan to refute by more evidence to the contrary. Voice tones change. Volumes increase, but you can't hear the difference. In the game of "never wrong" there can be no winners, only losers. When you are "never wrong," there is no discussion or compromise. It is now a battle that will never end.

Reflection:

Ask yourself what lurks behind the power-driven argument that is compelling you to such an immovable position. We have all known the pain of being right for all the wrong reasons. The point we are trying to make may be true and potentially valuable to our partner, but only if they want it. They are not going to embrace an idea that causes them pain at the hands of the messenger.

Prayer:

God, help me to understand that all of us have access to your will and I have not been charged with being the messenger to others.

The Faces We Wear-Part 1

Joker

Challenge:

Those who have learned to escape reality by playing the role of the fool wear the face of the "joker". The person who makes jokes when the situation is fraught with pain and sorrow is not acting out of disrespect or disregard for the suffering of others. It is simply a way of coping with emotional discomfort. The joker will frequently miss the cues that others find the humor to be unwanted or inappropriate. Those who love the joker will frequently feel unfulfilled as they expect him/her to remain emotionally available during times of emotional challenge and he/she is fooling around instead. This lack of fulfillment will generally lead to resentment and emotional distance that serves only to increase the joker's level of anxiety and insecurity. This will usually generate more joking until an explosion occurs.

Reflection:

The role of the "joker" should not be confused with the display of humor during a fun loving moment. We need to learn to laugh at ourselves and with each other because we have known great pain. The "joker" however, is not having fun and is not poking innocent fun at him or others. The joker is uncomfortable and needing to run and is willing to make himself/herself out to be the fool to avoid detection. If you are the joker, help is possible, but you will need to understand that forced laughter is an illegitimate form of crying. Take the risk to let others understand that you are frightened of your inability to cope with the situation. If you love a joker, consider that your support and acceptance is of vital importance and that many of your behaviors can be seen as rejection to one with a fragile self-esteem.

Prayer:

God, help me to laugh when it is funny and to cry when I am sad. Help me to avoid judging those who do not feel they have permission to embrace the feelings of the moment and instead hide what they are feeling.

The Faces We Wear-Part 1

Peacemaker

Challenge:

The "peacemaker" is a face that all of us have known in our recovery: "Peace At Any Price" was our motto, and what a price we have paid. We have led our mate to believe that we were supportive of his/her position when what we were really saying was "I am afraid to disagree with you." Those experiences of dishonoring ourselves would often bring praise from our romantic partner because we would be seen as cooperative, unselfish, and being willing to be a full partner. But were we really? If you are able to satisfy everyone then you have no self.

Reflection:

The path to freedom from the prison of "peacemaking" is one of the less traveled roads. It is easy to sit back and plot our revenge against the menacing forces in our lives like children imagining that, "One day, I will learn karate and make them all pay!" Although many of us were innocent victims as children, those of us who continue to blame the bullies in our life for the choices we are making now have learned to blame others for the quality of our own life. This is the road most traveled. We are doing far more than just blaming a bully for being a bully. This road leads to more pain and suffering and, in many cases, relapse. We must take responsibility for the quality of our own life in order to improve it. We are not the reason we were hurt as children. We are the reason that we hurt as adults. Involuntary conformity does not protect us from pain. It will help us forget what we stand for and drift from our Higher Power's grace, because we are "playing God" in the romance and deciding to give up ourselves to keep the peace. There can be no greater pain.

Prayer:

God, help me to be true to myself and to others as I go through my day. Help me to avoid harsh treatment and harsh retaliation towards others. Show me how to stand up for what I believe in without stepping on others. Help me to see how to take charge of the quality of my own life.

The Faces We Wear-Part 1

Power Player

Challenge:

The "power player's" role is characterized by an exaggerated desire to control the lives of others, as well as their thought processes. He/she is very much like the "actor" that the Big Book of *Alcoholics Anonymous* (1953) describes in the discussion on the 2nd Step on (pp. 60-61). The individual reliant on domination as a way of coping with life's inaccuracies and injustices generally attempts to control others without realizing it. If you love a "power player", you are familiar with the mood swings and periods of severe agitation when he/she cannot seem to get the world to correspond to his/her plan. If you are a "power player", you are not likely to admit it unless the price tag has been the perpetuation of the "insanity" that the 2nd Step addresses. If power dealing is a trap for you, do not give up - there is hope.

Reflection:

Alcoholics Anonymous (1953, p. 63) introduces the solution that establishes that the first requirement of surrender "is to be convinced that any life run on self-will can hardly be a success." The life of the "power player" is being run on self-will and little else. Although the "power player" may make others miserable in the process, it is not their goal. The "power player" is driven and can only feel comfortable when he/she is in control of all of the variables. It is a fear driven existence that will keep others from developing intimate and trusting relationships with him/her and will eventually lead to spiritual ruin. Most often the "power player" is not alone in the game. There can be no "power player" without a "peacemaker." The "power player" needs people to relegate the responsibility for the quality of their life to him/her in order to maintain power. If you want to help him/her give up the role, then take full responsibility for the quality of your own life.

Prayer:

God, help me to remember that I am not in charge of the emotional well-being of those I love. I cannot protect them from life's injustices; but I can protect them from me.

The Faces We Wear-Part 1

Truly Concerned

Challenge:

We believe that the "truly concerned" person looks to feel better about themselves and overlook their own shortcomings by speaking of the affairs of others. Most "truly concerned" people will claim to be solely concerned with the welfare of the person about whom the discussion is centered. In the name of "caring and sharing," some in our fellowship rooms will engage in the relating what we know or have heard about the shortcomings of others. "I knew that Harry was going to drink again, I am not surprised ...." "Did you see the way that Sarah was flirting at the workshop? It won't be long before she is relapsing again. I really feel sorry for her!" The journey of the "truly concerned" person can be well intentioned or intentionally hurtful but the destination will always be the same: the human spirit is injured. Both the spirit of the target of the "truly concerned" person and the emotional well-being of those passively involved in the gossip are threatened. The "truly concerned" person drifts away from the knowledge of a Higher Power's will for him/her by default.

Reflection:

Gossip as a means of communication is shallow. Gossip as a method of sharing concern is of no value to the person that the gossipers are "concerned" about. Gossip does not elevate your status and does not grant you immunity from the same shortcomings you are so quick to identify in others. If you talk about someone, instead of to someone, you are not showing concern at all. Gossip, like many of our faces, is a fear-based strategy for filling some void in us.

Prayer:

God, help me to be a reflection of your love in all that I do. Show me how to really love those I would judge through gossip. Help me to see in myself those defects which trouble me most about those for whom I care. Help me to pray for those I would judge whom I really have not cared about. Help me to have just one voice that would not be different if you sat by my side.

The Faces We Wear-Part 1

Weekend Workshop

As we began to examine our defects of character, we saw that we wore many different faces. For many years we held firmly to the notion that there needed to be different levels of honesty and openness or we would foolishly leave ourselves open to hurt. However well founded that belief may have been, given our respective childhoods, we assure you that it had to be abandoned. Like many of you, we too had hoped and prayed that the defects of character that laid the foundation for the games we played and faces we wore would be removed from us. Improvement in our overall functioning in relationships wrongly led us to believe that the work was done. The defects of character would, for the most part, have remained intact. The only difference was that we were "not as bad as we once were." Those famous last words, uttered by many of us when we were faced with flaws in our character, made it difficult to be honest with others and ourselves. Our journey throughout the 6th and 7th Steps opened our eyes to the fact that the faces that we wore kept us distant from each other and robbed us of the intimacy that we both desired.

John & Elaine

My Gifts to the Partnership

If you can identify with any of the five faces, write a letter to a God of your understanding about what you believe that face has cost you over the years. If you could not identify with any of the five, seek input from someone you trust for you are probably missing important information about yourself. Share what you discover about yourself with members of your support group.

Ask your partner if he/she would be willing to share what they have learned about themselves with you. Do not comment. Just listen prayerfully.

The Promises-Part 2

We Will Lose Interest in Selfish Things and Gain Interest in Our Fellows

Challenge:

When we were toddlers, the world, as we knew it was defined by what we could touch, smell, and taste. If it didn't make us feel good, we were not interested in it. If we couldn't experience it, then it didn't exist. For many of us, life prior to recovery was very much like the world of the toddler: we saw ourselves as the center of the universe. But we were not toddlers, and the world would not revolve around us. We could not get people to do as we wished. We could not maintain life as we wanted. *Alcoholics Anonymous* (1953, p. 61) describes us as a "self-seeker, even when trying to be kind." This is a path destined to leave us empty and alone. The right road, the one less traveled, would require that we become humble. It would require that we learn to derive pleasure and joy from service to others. When we grasp this concept of serving others, we immediately begin to feel this promise being fulfilled in our recovery. How often do you remember to include your romantic partner when you think of being of service to others? If we are going to "lose interest in selfish things and gain interest in our fellows," we will need to be focused on service to our fellows, especially our partner.

Reflection:

The problem lies in the misuse of our free will. True sobriety challenges us to use our God given will to be of service to our fellows. Initially, this is a difficult challenge for most of us because we fear that the outcome from our efforts of service will not be acceptable or fulfilling. Once again, we were blindsided by our instinctual desire to alter our own feeling states instead of keeping our eye on the needs of others, as our Higher Power would reveal it to us. Our Higher Power seldom needs for us to be concerned with the outcome. We only need to suit up and show up and he will do the rest.

Prayer:

God, help me to recapture the innocence and the wonder I had as a child without preoccupation with self. Show me how to be of service to you and all of my fellows through what I think, feel, say, and do.

The Promises-Part 2

We Will Intuitively Know How to Handle Situations Which Used to Baffle Us

Challenge:

We have all known regret about how we have behaved during times of uncertainty. Before recovery, we found that fear directed many of our actions. We allowed these feelings of fear and insecurity to dictate our behavior in ways that often damaged our self-esteem and important relationships. Each one of us has been given a map through these uncharted waters in the body of the 12 Steps. Through practicing the 12 Steps in all of our affairs, we have been shown ways of coping with situations that confused us in the past. Those of us engaged in committed relationships have known great ambivalence when we approached issues of intimacy and romance in our partnerships. In the past, we comforted ourselves by comparing our current relationship with past relationship failures or we tried to defend ourselves by bragging that our current partnership enjoyed great sexual fulfillment. These false reassurances often left us feeling unfulfilled, as they were quick fixes for a much larger problem. We had to admit our powerlessness and ask for guidance from a power greater than ourselves.

Reflection:

When we invite the God of our understanding in to guide us with our daily problems, all things are possible. This is how we right our relationships with our loved one. Quiet meditation and prayer is often all that is asked of us. Many of us stand ready to do, rather than to be. You can trust that when you open yourself up to the God of your understanding answers will come to problems that baffled you in the past. Look for ways to work the steps in your relationship and employ your partner as a member of your support system.

Prayer:

God, my desire is to let go of always having 'to do' rather than 'to be'. I understand that doing often distracts me from feeling your love and hearing your word.

The Promises-Part 2

The Fear of People Will Leave Us

Challenge:

During our active days, fear was in control and very little could be done to alleviate it. Addiction, in any form, could take the edge off for a while, but in the long run the "fixes" only generated more fear. Those of us who pretended not to be afraid ended up feeling lonely and misunderstood. If you reacted to this fear with behaviors aimed at controlling the people, places, and events in your life, you have known great disappointment and personal rejection. We each pay a different price for the ways we choose to eliminate our fear. Why must we eliminate it? It is just a feeling. It is not a fact.

Reflection:

The most damaging aspects of our fear are in the consequences we experience for attempting to deny it. Many of the conflicts that couples have brought to us have been based not in the fear, but in an unwillingness to expose it to each other. In recovery we have learned that once a fear has been shared it loses its power. A fear that is concealed arouses all the other fears we have experienced in the past. This "awakening" of fears associated with past traumas will leave many of us feeling overwhelmed and hopeless. Trust that your partner can handle your fears. If you keep your fears hidden, your partner will be injured by the method you use to keep them hidden. Your relationship cannot endure an infinite number of injuries. Eventually, even a relationship that is "of God" will cave in under the weight of the "secrets" that injure it.

Prayer:

God, during my efforts to share myself honestly with my partner, let me know that you are close by. I do not want to be afraid of the person you have given me to love. Help me to accept my fears as the awakening of feeling that can lead to the awakening of the spirit. Help me to remember that my fears lose their power when I share them.

The Promises-Part 2

Our Whole Attitude and Outlook Upon Life Will Change

Challenge:

Conventional thinking suggests that most of what we know about commitment and relationships are learned from our role models before we experience our first kiss. We have found that by age twelve, most children are preparing to graduate from "relationship college." With that picture in mind, think back to the "relationship college" you attended and the visions that were created which portrayed a happy relationship. Scary, isn't it? Most of us readily accept that our attitude and outlook upon life will have to change if we are to maintain sustained sobriety. But how many of us are willing to challenge our childhood notions of what it would take to have a fulfilling and challenging relationship?

Reflection:

The spiritual path we have chosen offers many challenges which most of us accept as dues we must pay for the improved quality of life that we seek. Those challenges are faced every day with our fellows through the use of the 12 spiritual principles we have been given. In meeting after meeting, we learn tolerance, patience, and acceptance. In the rooms of our respective fellowships, we have learned to view the glass of life as half full rather than half empty. In the coffee shops our recovering membership frequent, there is warm and compassionate conversation about topics we once became embroiled over. If we practice the principles of recovery in all of our affairs, we will have the same positive glow, even in our romantic relationships! Our attitude and outlook with regard to our romantic partnership will change if we are willing to challenge what we learned in "relationship college."

Prayer:

God, help me to be a student of my relationship. Foster in me the desire to bring the spirit we shared in the coffee houses of recovery into the living room with my partner.

The Promises-Part 2

Fear of Economic Insecurity Will Leave Us

Challenge:

The fear of economic insecurity can, as we have explored previously, penetrate every area of our lives. In a romance, the fear can take a variety of forms at different times of the year and at different stages of our development. Many of us experience an unnecessary sense of failure in our recovery when a fear that we were sure was removed seems to have returned. We are sure that the cause is a "faulty program" or a "partner who does not understand." The fear of economic insecurity is a wake-up call from our Higher Power. Changes might need to be initiated, but the fear does not mean that there is some failure to be ashamed of. No one has to be blamed. It is just a feeling, not a fact. If our Higher Power is calling us to get our attention, all we need to do is answer the phone.

Reflection:

Our economic future will be more a product of what we do today than what will be done to us at some point in the future by unknown forces. If we are living outside of our means today, that can be changed. Now is the time for action, not worry. If we need to earn more because life challenges require that we change our budget, we can find ways of earning more or spending less. Avoid judgment of self or others and do something. Tell yourself the truth about the shortfall, develop a plan for change, and monitor the plan to see where amendments are needed. Avoid living in the future for it can become a self-fulfilling prophecy.

Prayer:

God, help me to hear when you beckon me to look up and examine the path that I am on. Show me the changes that I need to make, and give me the courage to share the responsibility with the partner you have given me to remind me of the depth of your love for me.

The Promises-Part 2

Weekend Workshop

The "promises" as described on pages 83-84 in the Big Book of Alcoholics Anonymous (1953) have been a staple of our individual recoveries. We hope you have enjoyed our introduction to a way of using them in your relationship.

We have seldom seen a recovering relationship succeed unless both partners were actively involved in the practice of a 12 Step program. The "promises" offer a way of monitoring the spiritual progress of the relationship.

The recovery text Alcoholics Anonymous (1953) commits that these "promises will always materialize if we work for them (p. 84)." This theme will hopefully assist you in the evaluation of your efforts.

John & Elaine

My Gifts to the Partnership

Write down the actions you take to work toward the fulfillment of the five "promises" covered in this week's theme.

Write down the actions you take that block the fulfillment of the five "promises" covered in this week's theme.

Seek permission to share your writing with your partner. Do not solicit input from your partner about what you have written.

If your partner chooses to share his/her writing with you, offer no comment or identification; just listen.

Love Is...

More than a Feeling

Challenge:

Many of us have found ourselves in a debate over the difference between "loving someone" and "being in love with someone." When "in love," we are sure of our feelings and certain that we have found Mr. or Ms. Right. We believe that the relationship will last forever: "This is someone that I am in love with. All the others I only 'loved'!" All too often Mr. Right turns out to have personality flaws that are unacceptable. Ms. Right is not the understanding woman I thought she was. We find ourselves "still loving" him or her but not "in love with" the person.

Reflection:

That feeling of being "in love with" someone is a powerful emotion that will often leave us blinded and unable to learn from our past mistakes. We had, in the past, fallen in and out of love so fast that it would appear to be like the mood swing one would expect from a drug. And so it was. Consider the notion that there is really no difference between "loving someone" and "being in love with someone," and much of the confusion you have had regarding romantic commitment will begin to fade. "Being in love with" is a feeling which has hormonal and neurological origins as well as a basis in euphoric recall. It is grand and wondrous and can motivate us to take both productive and unproductive risks in our recovery. But it is just a feeling, it is not a fact. It becomes dulled, at times, by the work of addressing our compatible defects of character. In the past, when the feeling of "being in love" lost its luster, we would move onto the next relationship. It is time to stay where we are until leaving is not the solution to the feeling of dissatisfaction that often replaces "being in love."

Prayer:

God, help me to enjoy the fullness of romantic love complete with its thrills and spills. Help me to learn about myself in the relationship that I am in, rather than fantasize about how all will be right when I find Mr. or Ms. Right.

Love Is...

A Decision

Challenge:

Many of us have been damaged by earlier relationships with our parents or other people who have influenced our lives and our view of love. Through our life experiences, we may have learned that it is easier to avoid a serious commitment with another than it is to risk emotional discomfort. In the past, we made a choice – conscious or unconscious – to run from our mate. We may have said the words, "I love you and will be there for you forever," but, in truth we allowed fear to make our decisions and did not honor this commitment. In our efforts to protect ourselves, we created emotional barriers and designed escape hatches that prevented true intimacy. We thought these obstacles would prevent hurt, but they often backfired.

Reflection:

If we love truly, we will get hurt. If the relationship is of God, we will get through it and grow stronger. We must make a complete commitment to our partner because, "half measures avail us nothing." There is no justification for the injuries we have suffered in the past from those who claimed to loved us. The emotional scars from past hurts are real, but unless you decide that this is all there is, the journey does not stop here. Instead, you can invite your mate to be a part of your healing process through the exchange of love. The greatest healing comes from the giving of love to another. The opportunities to love unconditionally are endless—do not waste any.

Prayer:

God, my romantic life can feel like an emotional roller coaster when I focus on what I need rather than what I can give to my partner. Teach me how to honor the sacred commitment I made to my lover.

Love Is...

Unconditional

Challenge:

All of us have known the pain of having to jump through hoops to win the approval of another person. As children, many of us heard direct and implied conditions associated with the love we sought from the adults in our lives. We would, at times, exhaust ourselves trying to get it right, but we could not because true love cannot have strings attached to it. A person is not more lovable because they finish all their dinner or get straight A's on his/her report card. Some of us have endured emotional and physical abuse that we were assured happened because we were loved by the abuser. Something deep inside of us yearns for love without condition, but we cannot force it to happen. Unconditional love cannot be bargained for or won. Love requires nothing from us except a willingness to accept it. If others will not give it, there is nothing we can do.

Reflection:

In our adult lives, we come to understand the need for unconditional love and anticipate that we will be offered it by those who claim to love us. When it does not materialize we are understandably hurt. When it is withdrawn, we feel rejected and look elsewhere, sometimes until we find another partner. Unfortunately, many are better able to detect when they are not receiving unconditional love than they are at knowing how to offer it to another person. The desire to give and receive unconditional love is a gift from your God that is easily developed when we decide to love those around us because of who they are, rather than love them for what they might become.

Prayer:

God, help me to accept the perfect love that you show me everyday. You love me because of who I am, not in spite of who I am. Show me to love others as you love me.

Love Is...

Until...

Challenge:

We need to think in terms of permanent relationships. The decision to love cannot be a temporary proposition. Many relationships begin with the idea of permanence, but the foundations they are built upon are weak and unreliable. The ever-rising divorce rate is an indication of just how unstable the marital architecture must be. Many of the couples that we have worked with come with an expectation that the therapist will cast the deciding vote on whether or not they should remain together. They have invested many years and tears into the relationship and do not want to abandon it without "trying everything, lest someone blame them for giving up too soon." Oftentimes, the relationship is in such disrepair that it cannot, in its current state, be saved. It must be rebuilt. Many find it easier to just find another partner.

Reflection:

We recently entered into a debate with colleagues that argued that marriages are too easily dissolved and that they supported legislation that would make it more difficult to get a divorce. We listened patiently while they posted the blame on culture, religion, and politics for the dissolution of the institution of marriage. Our contribution was brief: it is too easy to get married. If the love is going to last longer than the ink on the marriage license, the couple will need to explore both the breadth and depth of their partner. When a relationship is constructed during active addiction or codependency, the structure will collapse. If, however, the relationship is based on common spiritual values and a willingness to work at developing a new foundation of openness, unconditional love, and God-centeredness, a new relationship can be rebuilt out of the wreckage of our past.

Prayer:

God, help me to keep you in the center of our relationship. Help me to demonstrate my commitment to my partner through my work towards a love that will last forever.

Love Is...

An Act that Increases Self-Worth

Challenge:

The pain of unreciprocated love does not require a detailed description. We have all known the emptiness that comes when those we love do not share our bond. We agonize over the rejection and redouble our efforts at self-examination to determine what about us is unlovable to those we desire intimacy with. The pursuit of the cause of our apparent unworthiness can leave us miserably disconnected from the flow of love all around us. We wait for it to come from those we have determined it should come from. Our personal sense of worth erodes under the relentless pounding of our tide of discontent. True love includes communicating a sense of increased self-worth. If our relationship does not enhance our self-esteem, one or both of us is failing to recognize or communicate the worth of his/her partner.

Reflection:

Does your love leave your partner enriched? Does your love leave your partner more courageous, self-respecting, and hopeful? If not, evaluate the degree of emotional and spiritual energy you put into celebrating what is right about your partner. When we have gotten stuck in the emotional trap of faultfinding in our own relationship, we have learned to declare affirmatively that our partner is "perfect." From "perfect" we can find "good" and love is not lost in that moment. From "wrong," we can only find fault and love gets lost in the shuffle.

In sobriety you have a choice: you can either contribute to the enhancement of your partner's self-esteem or you can diminish it. We pray that you work toward the solution.

Prayer:

God, help me to be a part of the solution rather than the problem.

Love Is...

There were many times in the early days of our relationship when we ran from the commitment that "I love you" represents. We were afraid to get hurt; afraid to injure our partner; but most of all we were afraid that we could not change. Both of us had many failed romantic relationships before our marriage of thirty-three years. The simple reality that we discovered was there could be no hope, only failure, if we did not stop running from each other.

This week's meditations have hopefully provided you with a way of examining your individual commitment. We pray that you will take the time to identify and close the escape hatches that you may be maintaining in the ready position.

John & Elaine

My Gifts to the Partnership

Look at the ways that you might still be running from your partner and identify the thoughts you ponder, the feelings you experience, and the actions you take just before you run from your partner.

Share your discoveries with a member of your recovery support group.

Obtain your partner's permission to share one of the less threatening ways that you run and what your plan is for changing that behavior. Do not solicit input from your partner about what you have written.

If your partner chooses to share his/her writing with you, offer no comment or identification; just listen.

Let the Slogans Guide You-Part 2

Live & Let Live

Challenge:

If asked, many of us would deny that we want a partner who looks, thinks, and acts like us. We cry out that we want our partner to "be an individual with his/her own mind" and resent times that he/she does not "think for himself/herself." Often it is our own insecurity that seduces us into trying to mold our partner into our own image and likeness because we falsely believe that the problem is him/her. We tell ourselves that the problem is that he/she doesn't understand or act appropriately and use this excuse as an explanation for our own frustration. As a relationship matures, it is not uncommon for partners to drift apart when they have become so similar in profile that it is difficult to know one from the other. This has happened because one partner has decided to control the other, and the other partner has decided to release his/her power to the other. Our respective recovery programs ask us to "Live And Let Live." Our mate is not a carbon copy of ourselves, but rather a unique individual who brings characteristics distinct to himself/herself. Ask yourself if you have attempted to squelch the uniqueness of your partner to offset your own feelings of ineptness.

Reflection:

On our wedding day we exchanged marital vows that encouraged each of us to maintain those parts of us, which were unique to us, and to blend those parts that would make our union more durable. We had both feared the loss of individuality as we had both known oppression in the past. We found that our sense of self was greatly enhanced by the power of our coupleship. When we allow our mate to develop his/her own sense of worthiness by avoiding the trap of trying to mold him/her into what we believe we want them to become, we are exalting in our mate's uniqueness as God's child.

Prayer:

God, I pray for the courage and wisdom to live my life today following your plan for me. We all have our own journey in this life, and it is not my job to ascertain what my mate's journey is to be.

Let the Slogans Guide You–Part 2

Just for Today

Challenge:

We have all known times when the challenges faced by those we love seemed to have generated great discomfort for us. It is so easy to get stuck in the holes that others are trying to extricate themselves from. Many times, we will join them in the hole because we have put our own recoveries on hold in an effort to get our partner to a better place because we fear where they are headed. There has also been many times where we have helped our partner dig the hole they are in by attempting to control them. Our power-driven attempts to "help" have sometimes left our partner feeling helpless and impotent. It is not what we intended, but so often, a well-meaning intervention to "help" was secretly being fueled by our own insecurity or lack of personal fulfillment.

Reflection:

When those you love are stuck, ask if there is some way for you to be of assistance and listen to the answer with a spirit of openness. That openness must begin with the acceptance that you are neither your partner's Higher Power nor the "keeper of the relationship." This acceptance is easier to establish and maintain if you are continuing to live your life. If you place your life and recovery on hold to do damage control, you may end up being the one who needs first aid. Allow the people you love to live their own life without keeping score and you will avoid painful frustration and resentment. Just for today, continue to live your life as you struggle to allow your partner to live his/her life and you will be available to deliver emotional and spiritual aid when they are ready.

Prayer:

God, show me how to be an example of your love through a commitment to service my partner, generously, without keeping score. Give me the courage to allow those I love to have the benefit of their own experience as they come to know you better.

Let the Slogans Guide You-Part 2

Think, Think, Think

Challenge:

"Why on earth did I say that?" "How could I have been so insensitive?" Many hurtful dialogues between romantic partners began because one or both of the partners trusted their perception of "the problem." They were guided by their feelings to say and do things that could not be reversed once they were out. These thoughtless exchanges can produce lasting resentment and deep injury to the spirit of the relationship.

Reflection:

Please remember that your perception of reality is just a perception. It is a view of what is going on that is routinely influenced by past experiences that have little or nothing to do with the situation at hand. Think through what you are seeing. Think! Is your judgment impaired by fatigue, past hurts, personal defects of character, or an accumulation of hurts that have not been resolved and that you are currently overreacting to? If you are hurt, it is real and we agree that your feelings do not have to be proven. But, remember that your feelings are not facts. Think! Your hurt is real, but that does not mean that the cause of that harm is your partner. We have feelings, and, unless we explore their origin in depth, we are apt to attempt to legitimize them by accusing those we are closest to for causing the discomfort.

Prayer:

God, help me to better know myself. As my feelings are awakening, help me to understand the breadth and depth of experience that have given rise to them. Help me not to injure others when I am uncomfortable.

Let the Slogans Guide You-Part 2

First Things First

Challenge:

There is so much to do and so little time to do it! All of us have known the disappointment of wanting more out of life than it can deliver. We have also known the frustration of having life deliver more than we have ordered, or so it seemed. We have been "whelmed" many times in our recovery by the demands of life as we tried to determine what the priority should be. Where do we start? How will we endure? At times, the drone of life was deafening and the frustration of trying to manage "all the stuff" would leave us emotionally toxic and miserably ineffective. From time to time, we would manage to make things worse by looking for someone to blame.

Reflection:

Many of us are familiar with the saying, "God will not give you more than you can handle." While this biblical reference could, at times, be comforting, it usually stung when others offered it as a way out of our emotional confusion and physical exhaustion. We, like many, would compare our situation to others and consider God unfair in his assignment of "stuff" to cope with. We have come to believe that the statement is a spiritual axiom with two parts, not one. The first part, God will not give you more than you can handle, reflects our understanding of God as a loving and caring creator and guide. The implied second part contains the understanding that with our own free will, we can single-handedly create great havoc in our lives. We can generate, through our inaction or our self-will, much more "stuff" than we can handle, both as individuals and as a couple. When we are lost and crumbling under the weight of consequences of either our actions or lack of acceptance, we can reach out to our partner for help to prayerfully return to our God for direction on how to establish what is first. "First Things First" is always the same: Pray for the knowledge of his will for us and the power to carry that out.

Prayer:

God, we seek the knowledge of your will for us as a couple in all that we think, say, and do.

Let the Slogans Guide You-Part 2

Experience, Strength, and Hope

Challenge:

Alcoholics Anonymous (1953) describes resentment as the "number one offender" (p. 64). It destroys more alcoholics than anything else and "from it stems all forms of spiritual disease." There is little we can argue to the contrary. From resentments come spiritual deterioration and the loss of fellowship or partnership. Love cannot withstand ongoing resentment. We believe that the birthplace of resentment is the unfulfilled expectation that others will want the world to be ordered they way we believe is best. We impose our ideas, perceptions, or insights on others or allow them to do the same to us. If the contributions are acceptable, all is grand. If the contributions are not acceptable, resentment is born. How have we come to believe that we know what is best for others? Would we ask others to control us with their direction for living?

Reflection:

Many years ago one of the author's was introduced to a concept that could greatly reduce resentment generated by advice giving. This concept flew in the face of the usual protocol for sharing at 12 Step meetings we attended which supported free flowing advice giving and the solicitation of specific direction on remedying any number of intimate life problems. Occasionally some brave soul would attempt to remind the "mob mentality" that we should lead others by our own experience, strength, and hope, but they would be summarily dismissed by those who were sure they knew what was best. The concept for sharing at meetings was relayed to us by a much older member of the rooms at a fellowship picnic in her back yard. Her wisdom was simple: "do not ask for advice because you might get it and do not give advice because somebody might take it." The older member was Lois Wilson.

Prayer:

God, burden my heart when I attempt to impose myself or my ideas on others because I have known you to be a loving and accepting God and not an imposing bully. Help me to focus on sharing my experience, strength, and hope with my mate.

Let the Slogans Guide You-Part 2

Weekend Workshop

We have learned to love the slogans we once felt were over simplifications of very involved dynamics of recovery. Today, they appear to be full of wisdom and we find application for them everywhere we look. We hope you have taken up the practice of meditating on them through the reflections that we have shared this week. Their meaning changes with time, in the same way we hope all of your lives are.

John & Elaine

My Gifts to the Partnership

The slogans can be a great framework to use for daily inventory. Take the slogans from both Parts 1 and 2 and list them on a sheet of paper. At the end of the day review the list and check off those slogans that have accurately described your use of the tools of sobriety during the day.

Obtain your partner's permission to share one of the slogans that you believe they implement well in their life and explain what you admire about them. Do not solicit input from your partner about what you have written for yourself unless you can do so without debate.

Avoid making comparisons between their behavior in the past and present. Remain in the present.

Growth

Social Growth

Challenge:

Social growth requires that you are able to look past selfish desires and work towards group ideals or "for the greater good." The 1st Tradition of *Alcoholics Anonymous* (1953) is the first introduction for many of us to the idea of social consciousness. Many of us will struggle to move from the self-centered "I" to the support of a "common welfare." Some of us were raised in homes where one was expected to behave in a socially acceptable manner, regardless of what was going on inside the home. You learned to "put on a happy face" and "be polite" in order to obscure parts of you that might be seen as negative. Many of us entered the rooms with either a "smile" on our face or in full rebellion against established social norms. There was much for us to learn about social maturity.

Reflection:

The 12 Step recovery programs offer us an opportunity to learn how to behave appropriately and honestly through guided study and positive role models. The guidelines and suggestions identified in the 12 Traditions provide a written guide for us to model and the seasoned members show us that change does not have to be drudgery. A newcomer quickly learns to listen more then he/she speaks. An observer at our meetings would probably notice how courteous and welcoming members are to one another. Would the same be said about you if you were observed in your home with your partner? Do you allow your partner to speak without opinion, judgment, or interruption? Are you courteous? Do you seek to be a member of the family group and a "trusted servant" rather than a leader? Many times we forget ourselves and treat those we love less respectfully than we would a newcomer to recovery. We can begin to change that by displaying common courtesies and looking for opportunities to be of service and to make sacrifices for our partner, much like we already do for others in our recovery group.

Prayer:

God, my desire is to become more socially competent in the way I treat others.

Growth

Intellectual Growth

Challenge:

Intellectual growth may seem like something beyond some of us and a preconceived reality for others. Intellectual growth involves the ability to make one's own decisions, with and without the counsel of others. There are many fear-based obstacles to the development of this degree of maturity in our recoveries that we generally encounter in our spiritual journeys. Intellectual growth involves the ability to have your thoughts challenged and changed when your mate has a better idea.

Reflection:

It is not easy to manage the levels of intimacy in our romantic relationships that are required if we are to be successful partners. We must be able to see our partner's input as valuable and be open to the changes we may need to make as a result of the insight we obtain from the sharing of his/her experience, strength, and hope. We must also be able to present input to our partner in a way that suggests that our perception is not fact and does not have to result in change. Mature intellectual sharing allows for healthy challenging of ideas and principles which we may have held sacred and vowed never to change. Remember, change is the only constant.

Prayer:

God, help me to take responsibility for being honest with my partner when asked for input and to be willing to receive his/her ideas without prejudice or prior contempt. Help me to share my insights in a loving and supportive way so that my partner can see I have prayed before I have spoken.

Growth

Emotional Growth

Challenge:

Most of us would recoil from input that suggested that we lacked emotional maturity. We may be a little hot-tempered at times or a bit thin-skinned, but we will not be accused of being immature. We must protect our honor, (we think), and we decide to defend ourselves, usually demonstrating that we are indeed emotionally immature. At one time or another, we have all known deep resentment because we were shunned by someone who we did not like. Why would we be upset about not getting invited to a party thrown by someone that we did not like? The leader fails to call on us at a meeting; we feel rejected, and the value that we might contribute to the discussion goes unrecognized. Our romantic partner is disturbed about something that we are certain has to do with us and we are deeply hurt when our efforts to "learn the truth" are thwarted by our partner.

Reflection:

Emotional maturity is a delicate balance between accepting emotions and keeping them under reasonable control. In the course of our respective recoveries, we have come to understand three important principles: 1) We do not have to act on everything we feel. We can be angry without becoming aggressive. 2) We are not necessarily entitled to an explanation for the actions and feelings of others and should not assume that we know what people mean unless we ask them. 3) While our feelings do not have to be justified or proven, we should not assume that our perceptions are accurate.

Prayer:

God, help me to take responsibility for the emotional quality of my own life. Whenever I blame others for how I feel, I drift from your grace and I will flounder at the mercy of others who would have to change to make me feel better. Help me to claim my feelings as my own. Show me ways of taking care of myself so I do not slip into the trap of believing that others are responsible for fixing me.

Growth

Romantic Growth

Challenge:

Many of us enter romantic relationships because of what we view as the relationship's potential. We see flaws and the potential for problems, but we diminish our fears by assuming that time will take care of the difficulties. We are uncomfortable with the recurring themes that surface in our arguments and accept shallow explanations for troublesome patterns like, "opposites attract" and "just work your own program and everything will turn out fine." Romantic maturity requires that we face the problems in our relationship regardless of how much time we have invested. The problems you choose not to face may very well become the relationship's undoing.

Reflection:

It is easy to move on to the next relationship when the one you are in gets to be a lot of work. Many times, couples we see in therapy tell us that the romantic flirtations they engage in outside of the relationship are innocent and harmless. If you want to experience the rich rewards of romantic maturity in your sobriety, then you will need to be committed to be in only one romantic relationship at a time. Flirting is defined as: "to amuse oneself in playful amorousness." That may still seem harmless unless you understand that "amorous" is defined as "strongly attracted to love, especially sexual love." How is that innocent? It is not – it is a silent killer of romance. When I am flirting with someone, I am pretending to be in a romantic relationship with that person. If I can only be in one honest romantic relationship at a time, than I must be "cheating" on my partner. You decide.

Prayer:

God, help me to remain in the moment. I long to see the fullness of your love in my romantic relationship with my partner. Help me to remain in the relationship that I am in at the moment so that I can grow and mature.

Growth

Sexual Growth

Challenge:

We grew up believing that sexual satisfaction and fulfillment could be realized and grow independent of romance and intimacy. We were raised in cultures that held that sexual desire and ultimately satisfaction were rooted in instinctual urges and physical attraction. We observed many marriages in the families around us whose romantic luster seemed to fade along with what was reported to be a diminished sexual desire. We did not understand, as we do today, that sexual desire is more likely to fade because of diminished romantic and emotional intimacy.

Reflection:

We had expectations galore about what each of our sexual duties and entitlements were. These expectations had, in large measure, been formed by the various media campaigns that promoted sex appeal above all other forms of human attraction. Like many, we could not measure up, so we purchased the stuff that we thought would level the playing field. We went to the places that the beautiful people frequented believing we would catch what they had. We gathered romantic conquests like notches on a gun belt, but the promise of fulfillment never materialized. Sexual prowess could not make one whole. The fulfillment we sought would come only after both of us were whole as individuals. Sexual fulfillment could only then be a part of that fulfillment. Sex was a poor substitute for intimacy, but now enhances the intimacy that we have developed.

Prayer:

God, show me how to love with the body that you have given me. Help me to be enough. Show me the importance of taking responsibility for caring for the body that you have given me. Provide me with opportunities to find peace in my struggle to gain freedom from the tragedies I have known in life. I want to be all that I can for my partner. Please help me to avoid taking responsibility for my partner's sexual and romantic happiness.

Growth

Growing up is hard to do. This week's themes reviewed some of the areas that we needed to grow up in. Our approach to romance and commitment was emotionally immature and spiritually weak. We came to trust that, with our God's help, we could learn from each other. We still have much to learn, but the journey is no longer frightening. We spend far less time making amends to each other because we spend much more time working on our defects of character.

John & Elaine

My Gifts to the Partnership

Write about the area of your romantic life where you have developed the most maturity in your recovery. Identify in your writing what ideas and behaviors had to be given up for you to begin to see measurable growth.

Share your discoveries with your God and a trusted friend or sponsor.

Obtain your partner's permission to share your writing with him/her. Do not solicit input from your partner about what you have written for yourself, unless you can do so without debate.

Avoid discussing what growth is still needed.

The Faces We Wear-Part 2

What If

Challenge:

To this question (rooted in anxiety and worry), our sponsors would suggest that we need to "turn it over." When we bring the problem up at a discussion meeting, the topic is likely to evolve into "Let Go And Let God," but that does not seem right. Isn't it normal to worry about something you care deeply about? Isn't it appropriate to worry about the welfare of someone you love? Worry, we think, is a duty—not an option. In fact, in some families it is a symbol of "love." After all, just how much could we really care if we did not worry about a loved one that was undergoing surgery or facing a significant emotional challenge?

Reflection:

The person who wears the face "What If?" would probably feel guilty about not being able to manipulate a situation, so they worry rather than seek help for themselves. Each of us has known the emotional challenges associated with being powerless over the fate of a loved one or the frustration that consumes us when a desired outcome is not forthcoming. It is difficult to accept that we may not get what we want for others, or ourselves but we must realize that worrying does not get us closer to the object of our desire. If you are worried about your partner: pray, serve, and accept support from others. Do not sit around and ask, "What If?"

Prayer:

God, help me to take the actions that I can and leave the outcome to you and my partner. I can only change myself and worry is a poor excuse for not wanting to accept, that which is out of my control. Please show me my place in the world. I have gotten much too big.

The Faces We Wear-Part 2

The Flirt

Challenge:

People who play the game of life wearing the face of the "Flirt" are unwilling to pay the price of being real. "The Flirt" is only pretending to be in a relationship and can never be sure of the other person's true feelings. They look to attract others with their physical self, rather than their emotional and spiritual self. These conquests are usually of little value. The female who feels that her body defines her will attract men with little depth who are likely to run away from a true relationship. The men who collect women like trophies will generally find that they are shallow and disloyal. He may have "bagged" the trophy with the intent of feeling more secure, but he is likely to be left feeling *less than*.

Reflection:

If we are to develop a mature and lasting romantic relationship that is mutually rewarding and serves to enhance the life of our partner, the price will be high. We must be willing to follow the course of self-disclosure, which allows our partner to experience and appreciate the aspects of us that are not merely sexual. If we are to move beyond the crippling effects of our insatiable appetite for sexual security, we will need to be willing to explore our partner's innermost being. When these practices are commonplace, the sexuality of our relationship will grow in richness and excitement.

Prayer:

God, help me to remember that my body is a vehicle. It is a way to express love, not the center of all love. I have known great sadness and lack of fulfillment pursuing security in sexual conquests. Help me to develop the balance that reduces my insecurity and increases my reliance on you.

The Faces We Wear-Part 2

Resentments R Us

Challenge:

We are cautioned at every turn to avoid the trap of resentment but many of us will fail to heed the warnings when we become preoccupied with finding somebody or something to blame for the quality of our lives. Resentment is rooted in a loss that we are unwilling to accept. This process begins with the belief that we are entitled to have some event or relationship turn out differently. Our anger grows (along with its cousins, cynicism and sarcasm) to the point that others are injured. We think our anger is justified by the injustice we have experienced.

In our romantic relationships, resentments are often still smoldering from perceived wrongs done to us by our current and past partners. It is quite common for perceived injuries from several past relationships to pour into the boiling caldron of emotion we are brewing for our current partner.

Reflection:

Our feelings are caused by our own emotional response, our own choices and our own behavior. Those who wear the face of "Resentments R Us" are reactors, not actors; eventually, when they realize this, they are left with no remnant of self-respect. We have all known disappointment and rejection, but the resentful person has felt the anguish of not getting what they "deserve" for so long that they become their own disappointment. We can grow wiser or hardened by our life experiences–the choice is ours.

Prayer:

God, help me to let go of the outcomes long enough to honestly examine my role in my own unhappiness. Show me how to look in the mirror for the answers I seek. Guide me as I go out from here to try and ease the burden of others.

The Faces We Wear-Part 2

The Procrastinator

Challenge:

People who wear the face of "The Procrastinator" will put off what he/she finds to too uncomfortable to face today. We have all tried our hand at the avoidant game of procrastination and suffered whether we had a winning or a losing hand. When we delay the work of the moment to alleviate our fear of failure or to avoid discomfort, we are setting the stage for disappointment.

So often in romantic relationships, we injure those we love because we do not carry our fair share of the load. We mean to, but other seemingly more important things get in the way. We assume that the needs of the relationship or the desires of our partner can wait. When we disappoint those who thought they could depend on us, we regret our delay and promise to get it right next time. But next time it is often the same. Fear, discomfort, and preoccupation with self set the groundwork for procrastination to take hold like a sickness.

Reflection:

We have listened to the discouragement of many clients who have felt that the very foundation of trust was being threatened by their partner's seeming inability or unwillingness to follow through with commitments. Many of us have had to bear great shame because we could not be counted on. Our word and our intentions meant nothing because those we loved were watching our actions that were frequently too little, too late. You alone have the power to show those you love that you can be counted on. Turn shame into action and it will restore your dignity.

Prayer:

God, help me to be true to your will, true to myself, and true to my word.

The Faces We Wear-Part 2

The Parent/Sponsor

Challenge:

The romantic partner who wears the face of "The Parent/Sponsor" could be playing a very dangerous game that is not motivated by a genuine, healthy, and mature love. There are three possible causes: (1) a self-serving desire to preserve his/her own security by controlling his/her mate's behavior (2) a self-serving desire to keep his/her mate dependent on him/her (3) a dependent response to his/her mate's desire to relinquish responsibility for the quality of his/her own life to the parents/sponsor.

Reflection:

The practice of "separate programs of recovery" should not mean that one's partner should have no input into the recovery process that they are sharing with the other. Yes it is true that we should not be in charge of our partner's recovery; however, we should play an active role in our partner's recovery as an intimate member of his/her support group. No one is apt to be better equipped to know when you are in trouble than your partner. The problem comes when you think you know what is best for your partner. It is dangerous to have the "knowledge of God's will for others."

Prayer:

God, help me to keep the focus on our romantic relationship so that our children can continue to benefit from the peace and love of our sacred union.

The Faces We Wear-Part 2

Weekend Workshop

The faces that we wore were originally intended to keep us safe from harm. In the beginning they did just that. Now we find that the hiding that used to be a survival tactic is no longer safe—it is dangerous. During this weekend workshop we will ask you to examine the costs.

John & Elaine

My Gifts to the Partnership

If you can identify with any of the five faces we chose for this week, write a letter to God about what you believe that face has cost you in your current relationship. Share what you discover about yourself with members of your support group.

Ask your partner if he/she would be willing to share what they have learned about themselves with you. Do not comment. Be a student.

Prayer of St. Francis-Part 2

That Where There Is Doubt, May I Bring Faith

Challenge:

It is so easy to become mired down in the fear and doubt that can infect a relationship. Prior to your current relationship, you and your partner may have developed many reasons for not trusting romantic commitments. It is difficult for many of us to work through the fears that tell us that the future will end up like the past. What are we to do with the ghosts that haunt us in our current relationship when we have taken all the actions suggested to us and the fear remains?

Reflection:

It can surely be a struggle to put one foot in front of the other when fear is taunting us from the darkness. The struggle will be lessened if you share it with your partner. Do not look for reassurances. Do not formulate tests to assess your partner's commitment. Do not believe that you know what your partner is thinking or feeling. Bring the fear that you have to your partner and share it. When you share the fear it will loosen its grip on you. Your partner does not need to have a solution - just a shoulder to lean on and the experiences that they have had. Faith will be born. We promise.

Prayer:

God, show me where I can bring faith where there is doubt. Help me to accept that the fears my partner has are real and have a genuine basis in some reality even though it may have occurred before we met. I want to share the faith that I have in the journey that You are guiding us through. Help me to be gentle and reassuring.

Prayer of St. Francis-Part 2

That Where There Is Desire, May I Bring Hope

Challenge:

You will be able to see when your partner is in despair no matter how hard he/she may try to hide it. Determining how to be of service when your mate appears to be sinking can be very difficult. Many times we react out of fear and approach our partners with judgment and criticism, perhaps telling them that they are stuck and not doing what we think will lift them out of it. There are also times that the pain of what is happening to them causes us to want to run away in search of what we have come to call "feel goods." These diversions into excesses of food, sex, and material possessions only create more confusion and despair. They generate our partner's mistrust in us. When we run to "feel goods," our partner will become (rightly) suspicious that we cared about their pain only because it was bothering us, not because of our empathy.

Reflection:

If we can meet our partners in their spiritual desert we may be able to be of service. The hope St. Francis suggests we offer can come though our willingness to simply meet our partner where she/he is and support them with understanding, identification, and prayer. We do not need to have a solution to the problem. The solution to the problem will come when we stop contributing to the problem by trying to wish it away. Your risk will be rewarded with the cutting of a new road through the wilderness.

Prayer:

God, help me to see the entrance when I can feel only thorns. You know that I get frightened when the people that I love are in pain. Help me to stay put. Help me to offer what comfort I can through your love and example. Take from me the burden of feeling responsible for changing the circumstances that I believe are causing the problem. I know that our journey through the deserts of life will always lead to safety.

Prayer of St. Francis-Part 2

That Where There Are Shadows, May I Bring Light

Challenge:

We all have experience with the burden that is created by what we believe to be a need to maintain secrets in our relationships. We might be keeping secrets that others have told us that we do not have the right to divulge to our partner. If secretive material surfaced in our 4th Step, are we obliged to share those with our partner? We will have to rectify that pain with God if we hear in meditation and counsel with our support system or spiritual advisor that the revelation of the secret will injure our partner. How do we know what the next right thing to do is?

Reflection:

Your partner is likely to be the one person in your life most capable of knowing when you need help or the person most aware of when you are slipping back into willfulness. We have often spoken about the benefit of having your partner become an active part of your support group. The price for this benefit of a stronger support group is honesty, as always. The secrets you keep about your defects of character, unmet social, emotional, and sexual needs, and the shadow cast by silent scorn can undermine your very best efforts at developing and maintaining a healthy romance. The only way to change is to change.

Prayer:

God, help me to step out of the shadows and into the sunshine of your love. Help me to reveal myself to my partner in a way that will enhance the emotional, spiritual, and sexual aspects of our relationship.

Prayer of St. Francis-Part 2

That Where There Is Sadness May I Bring Joy

Challenge:

So many of us come into our respective programs with deep sadness and grief over the losses we have suffered from our addiction. We walk into the rooms full of despair and fear that we suspect will be with us always. The illness with which we were afflicted had robbed us of the feeling of personal security and we nervously sought ways to fill the hole inside of us. Unfortunately for most of us, we sought comfort in all the wrong places. Some engaged in a new relationship, looking for the other person to fulfill the loneliness and despair. Others sought comfort in obsessive behaviors such as overspending, compulsive eating, or uncontrollable rehashing of thoughts and repetitive behavioral patterns. What we eventually learned is that these substitutes/behaviors are only temporary patches that could never fill the hole inside of us. The patch created a larger hole as its edges frayed and the novelty of the new "toys" wore off. We felt we were working hard at the business of recovery but the return on our investment seemed to be shrinking rather than growing.

Reflection:

The sadness and fear we feel in the beginning is real and we must embrace those feelings or their grip will become crippling. We can do this first by acknowledging them and then by sharing our pain with another person (possibly our partner) and allowing the sadness to wash over us. We have a choice. Do we continue to seek quick fixes to our emotional pain thereby blocking our chances for healing and progress? Or, do we surrender to our sadness and allow our Higher Power and others to restore us to sanity? Personal joy and contentment is available to each of us. We can begin this process by getting out of our own way and serving others. As we serve others, we will find that our own sense of well-being and happiness returns.

Prayer:

Dear God, once again I find myself focusing on what I believe I need and must have in order to feel whole. Please show me the truth.

Prayer of St. Francis- Part 2

Lord Grant that I May Seek Rather to Comfort, than Be Comforted

Challenge:

When we are hurting, we long to be comforted. We identify those people who we believe should know how to make it better and resent them when they fail to meet our needs. We assume that others, if they loved us, would be able to read the cues we are sending for help. When they do not respond, we get angry and judge that they really do not love us. We pound and pound on the drum expecting that life (if it were fair) and God (if he were just) would send a deliverer. We are consumed with self and relapse begins to loom on the horizon, even though we might not be able to see it.

Reflection:

Everyone will know times of deep sadness when there seems to be no deliverance possible. Either the people who have tried to help us are the "wrong ones" or the interventions they have offered do not work. There appears to be no way out. St. Francis and the 12 Step fellowships suggest a clear way out of the unending pain: be of service to others. Without service to others the vent intended to relieve us of the burden of preoccupation with self will become clogged and despair will soon follow. Your pain will have purpose when you use it as a basis for helping another.

Prayer:

God, show me how to serve others in all I do, especially when I am consumed with my own needs and wants.

Prayer of St. Francis- Part 2

Weekend Workshop

The Prayer of Saint Francis has been a source of restful reflection for us for many years. The author clearly understands the struggles we have faced. We find the challenges it presents both humbling and invigorating. We are humbled by the imperfection that we identify in ourselves and invigorated by the sense of hope the prayer conveys to us. We can change if we know where we have been and where we are going. When we accept the truth about ourselves, the gates are opened. We hope that this week's meditations have helped you to bring the prayer into your romantic relationship to use as a monitor for the relationship's romantic health.

John & Elaine

My Gifts to the Partnership

Examine the aspects of your life that you are lacking hope in and write about the fears that have drained the hope from your reserves. Share your discoveries with a member of your support group.

Reflect on the times that your partner has been provided for with your comforting. Share your recollections with him/her.

Building Trust

Managing the Ghosts of Our Past

Challenge:

Most of us developed, after conception, in a warm and soothing, self-contained environment which automatically fulfilled our every need. At birth, things were going to change drastically and there would be no preparation. For most of us, the birthing experience was quite hostile: goodbye nurturing womb, hello antiseptic delivery room. We had no choice but to trust our caregivers.

Many of us were unfortunately going to continue experiencing a world that was in many ways untrustworthy. Much of what we saw and experienced was to be sworn to secrecy. So secret, in fact, that we would learn to deny that we experienced anything. We were discouraged from expressing unpleasant emotions.

What was the truth? Who could we trust? To those questions and many others we heard: "You will understand when you are older." We got older and we still did not understand.

Reflection:

The challenges associated with developing trust in a romantic relationship can feel overwhelming, but they can be overcome. First, you must develop a personal understanding of the life experiences that have shaped your beliefs and rules regarding trust. Be honest with yourself about what others have done and gentle with yourself for having endured it. Be honest about your wrongs and gentle with the people that once endured your defects of character. Many of our beliefs about trust were formed long before we met our current mate. It is important to develop a working knowledge of the rules that we are using to decide how much to trust in our current relationship. Many relationships have unfortunately experienced painful wounds caused by infidelity and abuse of various forms. Healing is possible if both of you want it.

Prayer:

God, help me to first develop my understanding of your love for me. From that love, which is unconditional, I may learn to trust others and risk exposure.

Building Trust

Exposing the Obstacles to Trust

Challenge:

If you have examined the basis for your mistrust, then you have had an opportunity to reflect on a number of rejections that you have experienced. Perhaps those rejections left you unsure of your ability to accurately read people. Sometimes the rejections seem to occur without warning. We were so sure of what was going on, or were we? The questions come like meteorites: What happened? How did I miss this coming? I should have known better! How could I have been so stupid? I'll never do this again! What did I do?

Reflection:

One particularly formidable obstacle to developing trust was embedded in our lack of trust in our own feelings. When you are suspicious of your partner's motives for a particular behavior, ask them what they are thinking and/or what they are feeling. Do not spend time analyzing the other person's behavior. You will frequently be wrong because you are attempting to interpret their behavior through your feelings that, although real, are not facts. If you are feeling lonely and want more attention, ask for it directly without playing games like: "If she really loved me…!" If you are interested in sex, discuss it openly rather than relying on "cute" flirtations that can be too easily misinterpreted. When you are feeling unlovable or unloving, let your partner know that there is something amiss so they are not left to misinterpret your behavior as a personal rejection. Trust what you feel and report it.

Prayer:

God, help me to be myself with my partner. I sometimes fear that he/she will not love me unconditionally as you do, but I have really not given him/her enough opportunity. When I get hurt, I give up and withdraw my trust. Show me how to place my trust in you when I want to run so you can carry me across the bridge of honesty.

Building Trust

Avoiding Score Keeping

Challenge:

When we are emotionally or spiritually blocked, we have the keenest insight into the ways in which others have harmed us. We can remember exactly how many times our partner has failed to keep a promise. We know how often the sacrifices we have made for our partner have not been reciprocated. We are certain that our track record reflects continued emotional and spiritual progress and have evidence to support our position that our partner has stopped "doing the deal."

We think that our partner needs to earn our trust. While it might be true that our partner has harmed us and we are fearful, the proof of their trustworthiness will require that we be prepared to take risks that we might be disappointed again. There is no trust without risk.

Reflection:

If our energy is spent in the pursuit of justice and what is fair, we will have to become very good at keeping score. The trouble with being the keeper of justice and the watchdog of fairness is that we are generally unable to afford the bill. We make decisions of whether or not we can trust our partner based on his/her past track record, but what about our own? Beware of the tendency to identify the actions of others as warranting your mistrust when your own behavior is dismissed as being impulsive or forgetful. Building trust in a relationship requires risk taking. You will need to take the risk that you partner is growing and your partner will need to take the risk that you have grown.

Prayer:

God, help me to see what I owe instead of developing a case against those who I have found to be unworthy of my trust. Help me to accept those that do not want to change without harming myself with expectations that they will be different. Help me to accept the commitments of those that desire to grow and show me ways that I can be of service to them rather than devising methods for testing their sincerity.

Building Trust

Testing Always Requires Further Testing

Challenge:

"If you loved me...!" How many times have you cringed when you heard that injunction used to explain that you have disappointed a loved one? When we hear those words, we generally feel either fear or anger. Fear develops as we consider that we have failed to honor yet another commitment to our partner. Anger boils when we suspect that there is no way of ever satisfying our partner. When anger and fear are mixed and you allow the mixture to ferment, you will distill guilt. But, as we have seen many times before, guilt is a good short-term motivator and a lousy fix to a problem whose core is lack of commitment. Even though we have resented the trials we have been put through by others, we have each been "guilty" of testing our partner's commitment. We have kept our needs or desires a secret and then judged our partner for not meeting our needs.

Reflection:

Testing a person's love, honesty, or commitment only leads to more testing. When we have developed a scheme for evaluating our partner's love, honesty, or commitment, we have undoubtedly done so through manipulative means. The results of the test are always going to be inconclusive because we are being dishonest and are apt to suspect that the change we had desired is only temporary, or only a reaction to the ultimatum or manipulation we have used. We must construct another way of knowing the truth about what our partner is thinking or feeling. The "ATP test" is well researched and very user-friendly. You do not need any scientific tools; you need only have the courage and "Ask The Person" what you want to know. If you are receiving the truth, you will know it. You will gain access to the deeper truths you seek when you are more revealing of yourself and express an honest desire to get to know your partner better – without expectation that insight will result in change.

Prayer:

Help me to prepare my partner for honesty by demonstrating it myself.

Building Trust

Trust Does Not Take Time, Only Willingness

Challenge:

The most common obstacle to trust is maintenance of the erroneous perception that trust takes time. We enter a relationship and move slowly in the disclosure of our personal self because we believe that moving slowly will prevent us from getting hurt. We sometimes move slowly because we do not want to scare our prospective partner away because he/she has difficulty trusting others. We have all known romantic rejection in the past that has left us either rebounding blindly into the next relationship or declaring that we will never trust again. It would seem that we must cultivate trust through a series of shared experiences that support or diminish our perception of our partner's trustworthiness. But how much time should that take? Should we know each other for 2 years before we commit? Can we commit to trusting before we know all of our partner's secrets? What are we waiting for—a failure on the part of our partner? Yes, we think that is the case and perhaps that is not such a bad idea.

Reflection:

Many of us have had the idea that loving and trusting is only possible when we can be assured that we are not going to get hurt. We believe that hurt is inevitable when you are engaged in a loving and trusting relationship. Hurt is inevitable because trust-building requires self-disclosure and self-exploration. When we fail our partner or our partner fails us we will begin to understand what we are both made of. We will, through our failures, learn to be in a committed relationship. Trust does not take time. Trust takes a decision. The decision each of you made to open up to strangers in your respective fellowship developed a bond between you and others very quickly. It did not take time – just a decision to either expose yourself or let someone else in.

Prayer:

God, help me to share myself freely with others without regard for reciprocation. Help me to take the risk to let my partner see me when I am my most vulnerable and unlovable self.

Building Trust

We came into our relationship with many reasons to not trust a romantic partner. Prior to our current romantic relationship, the emotional states of rejection, betrayal, and abandonment where common for both of us. Making a decision to trust each other was very risky. We would need to avoid playing the games of our respective pasts that we thought had protected us from harm. The reality is that we were hurt just as much when we avoided love, as we were when we took a risk. The walls we had erected around us kept both the love and hurt out; however, the hurt we felt from not having love remained within the walls we had constructed.

Please take a risk to love and be loved. You might get hurt but you will grow through it.

John & Elaine

My Gifts to the Partnership

Examine the steps you take or games that you play to try and prevent yourself from getting hurt. Pick a favorite of yours and create a balance sheet. On one side list the hurts that the game protected you from. On the other side of the sheet write about the love that it deprived you of.

Share with a member of your support group the game you have written about so they can call you on it in the future.

Share a game that you have played in the past that you have not played in your current relationship. Do not invite input.

Recovery Through Prayer

Daily Prayer & Meditation

Challenge:

The importance of daily prayer and meditation in the life of a recovering person is generally understood. Most of us recognize that regular communion with a "power greater than ourselves" is vitally important to our day to day physical, emotional, and spiritual well-being. The practice of daily prayer and meditation is equally important to the life of our romantic relationship. We have learned over the years that the bond of our relationship will easily fall victim to our individual wants, overbearing schedules, and projections about the future unless we have God in the center.

Reflection:

Your focus on the spiritual well being of the relationship is an appropriate exercising of your will. We hope that you will pay attention to the distractions created by your interest in the pursuit of economic security, social prestige, and sexual pleasure. These interests are not inherently bad. In fact, they would appear to be God-given. However, if they come before your relationship with your Higher Power, you are apt to lose the tie that binds you to your partner.

Prayer:

God, help me to keep perspective in my pursuit of the fulfillment of my natural instincts. Show me ways to meditate on the goodness and security I can derive from keeping you in the center of all of my relationships.

Recovery Through Prayer

The Serenity Prayer

Challenge:

We have found it to be much easier to practice the spirit of the Serenity Prayer in the less important and less intimate relationships in our lives. We have often counseled couples to look for an explanation for why their behavior at 12 Step meetings is different than their behavior at home. We have come to develop the wisdom to know the difference between what we need to accept and what we need to change much quicker in our relationships with our recovering fellows. However, in our relationship with our romantic partner where the stakes are much higher, we are slow to acquire the wisdom. Why is it that this guiding light of acceptance is so difficult to come by in the most important relationships?

Reflection:

The serenity to accept the things we cannot change is elusive in romantic relationships for many reasons. The greatest challenge for us has been the tendency to grant our partner a fairly narrow margin of error. We expected that loving should not include hurt. We were wrong. The courage to change the things we could seemed easier to do in the relationship's inception when we were thrilled by who we could become in this new partnership. When it became challenging, we were frightened and wanted to run. The wisdom to know the difference between what we could change and what we needed to accept came very slowly, which is silly since the discriminating factor was so clear. The only thing that we could change is ourselves. As long as we placed our happiness in the expectation that the other person would change we remained dissatisfied.

Prayer:

God, help me to see me more clearly. Help me to take the focus off my partner and place it on you. The inspiration of the 11th Step, which is to seek to better understand your will for me, needs to include the enrichment of my understanding of how I am to serve you in my relationships.

Recovery Through Prayer

3rd Step Prayer

Challenge:

The 3rd Step Prayer, as it is commonly referred to, begins to clarify the purpose of the 12 Steps. Each of the steps is moving us closer toward the position of serving God and our fellows in all that we do. It has become known as the "surrender prayer" because it accompanies the decision to "…turn our will and our lives over to the care of a Power greater than ourselves." This decision is confined to the surrender of our choice to engage in our "substance" of abuse. That decision came in the 1st Step. The 3rd Step is intended to exclude nothing. Unfortunately, many of us have declared certain areas of our recovery "off limits." When we have done this the results were disastrous. Every time we decide to take back the control of our relationship and assert our individual interpretation of God's will for the other person we have paid a great price.

Reflection:

A decision to take the 3rd Step in our relationship, sometimes on a daily basis, was an action step. During the times we had the courage to pray about the health of our relationship, we were amazed with the insight we developed and the understanding we were blessed with. The decision to pray together was an action that opened the door to a God that loved for us to love each other. If the romance is being replaced by judgment, intolerance, and isolation, perhaps God has been locked out of your relationship. The key is in the 3rd Step prayer or any prayer you design to unlock the door.

Prayer:

God, help me to see that I am cheated by my decision to declare certain areas of my life "off limits" to your guidance and support. Help me to avoid playing God in my relationship.

Recovery Through Prayer

7th Step Prayer

Challenge:

The 7th Step Prayer, much like the prayer you have associated with surrender, is designed to increase your understanding of the knowledge of God's will for you and to broaden the scope of your service. We are asking to have our defects of character removed that "… stand in the way of" our usefulness to God and our fellows. Most of us would agree that our defects of character take the greatest toll on our lives in our most intimate relationships. However, we are the most reluctant to let go of the behaviors associated with those defects in the relationships which we are the closest to.

Reflection:

We have come to understand that our defects of character are the self-defeating remnants of tools that we once found great use for. At one time in our lives, our defects of character were assets or ways of coping with an unfriendly world. Today we understand that they greatly diminish the quality of our lives, but we can't seem to let go. The defects appear resistant to change because we attempt to remove the more severe aspects of the problem behavior without getting to the root. The only way to approach the root of the problem is to determine that I am ready to have my defects removed from all aspects of my life, especially in my romantic relationship.

With this humble beginning, we can honestly approach the 6th and 7th Steps.

Prayer:

God, help me to develop the courage to reveal my defects of character to my partner.

Recovery Through Prayer

11ᵗʰ Step Prayer

Challenge:

So often our romantic relationships have been undermined by our preoccupation with self. This can happen quickly and easily when we are feeling deprived of emotional, economic, or social security. When we are "hungry" in these ways, we place greater expectations on our romantic partners to "fill" us up. We are hurt when they refuse or their contributions fall short of our expectations. The Prayer of St. Francis can be a focal point that will help you get spiritually centered and will return God to the center of your relationship (in place of the entitlement that comes when we are centered on self).

Reflection:

The Prayer of St. Francis can be used to center your relationship if you are willing to examine each of the solutions that are presented. When you are emotionally or spiritually hungry, your partnership will be at risk. A steady diet of deprivation will always breed excess. We will begin to want more of one thing because we are hungry for another and can't seem to get what we feel we need.

The 11ᵗʰ Step Prayer provides a way for you to closely examine your own emotional and spiritual health. The questions that it poses will help you to evaluate the expectations you bring to your partnership. Your answers to the questions will provide insight into what you can change. It will offer you a way out of the bondage of self.

Prayer:

God, help me to better understand the impact of my emotional and spiritual deprivation on my partnership.

Recovery Through Prayer

Weekend Workshop

This week's theme has hopefully reinforced the use of prayer in your relationship. We have found it to be a vital tool, especially when we are feeling powerless and at a loss for what to do to comfort our partner. The prayers we have chosen have a common theme of change and service. We pray that you continue to address areas of needed change and look for opportunities to be of service to others.

John & Elaine

My Gifts to the Partnership

Use the prayers included in this week's theme as the basis for a twice a day meditation time.

Examine an uncomfortable feeling or experience that you had this week with your partner that left you confused about the motives behind his/her behavior. Imagine what life experiences he/she may have been exposed to that may explain the way he/she demonstrated the feeling he/she was having.

Explore the rules that you were exposed to as a child that may have influenced the way you deal with feelings today and share the memories with your partner. Examples: Big Boys Do Not Cry or Girls Do Not Get Angry. Ask your partner to pray with you when you are really disturbed about something that has occurred provided it does not have to do with them.

Let the Relationship Be of Service

To Children

Challenge:

Your first glance at this topic may have resulted in you thinking, "this isn't for me...I do not have any children." Before deciding this meditation is not for you, take a look at the various relationships you are in and identify the "children" that are part of your life today. This topic is not exclusive to those who have given birth, but to all who have an opportunity to impact the life of a child. We all have an opportunity to minister to children. It is not uncommon for adults to feel overwhelmed with the responsibility of parenting or mentoring children. They envision years of hard work with little guidance on how to embrace this daunting task. Our childhood memories, both the joys and sorrows, influence how we view this new experience. As we explore our own histories, we will gain a greater understanding of what we need to do to serve the relationship. Raising a child is an excellent opportunity for service. Do not let your fear or ignorance stand in the way. Embrace this experience as another gift from your Higher Power.

Reflection:

As adults, we need to embrace our powerlessness and accept that children are on loan to us for a short period of time. Our job is to guide and love our children during the time that we have with them. This is a challenging, but not unattainable, task to undertake. For those of us who were raised in families where children were not respected and cherished, we struggle with this task because we decide that "only the best" will do for our own children. We do not want our childhood histories repeated in the lives of the children we love. Our determination, although well-meaning, may block us from seeing how our insistence in making it "better" for our child may result in denying our child the opportunity to live his/her own life as intended. Both of us shared immense excitement and fear when we gave birth to our children. We began this journey believing we had the ability to shield our sons from physical and emotional pain. As you may expect, our attempts were futile. Our lesson was learned the hard way; our first child was born with a congenital heart defect that caused him to suffer extensively during his childhood. By the grace of God, we both came to understand that we were ill equipped to shield either one of our children from the problems they faced or would eventually face as they matured. Once we allowed God to parent our children, we were free to let go of the results. Our children were witnesses to our love for one another that gave them the strength and conviction to go forward and create their own story. Never underestimate the personal security your child will gain simply by witnessing the exchange of unconditional love between his/her parents. God will take care of the rest.

Prayer:

God, in the stress of parenting or mentoring, I forget that my responsibility is to serve children mainly by offering the security of a loving relationship. It is not my job to insulate him/her from the realities of life. I pray to willingly stand by to allow the love and wisdom of my child's Creator to care for him/her. Thank you for your gift of life.

Let the Relationship Be of Service

To Other Couples

Challenge:

As your romance deepens, you will take notice to the great number of troubled relationships around you. Some of the pictures you see will sadden you because of what you know: it is possible for the partners involved, if only they are willing, to take a risk to open themselves up to each other. Unfortunately, there will be relationships that are dear to you that you will see decay into a "tolerable arrangement" which are bound to end in separation. While it is true that you have no real power to effect a change in the pictures that you see, your relationship can be a beacon of hope to others if you let it shine.

Reflection:

The two of you will have many opportunities to be of service to other couples that will not require huge sacrifices. When a meeting topic develops around gratitude, take time to talk about your relationship and the ways in which sobriety has positively impacted it. When you and your mate are socializing with other recovering couples, avoid the tendency to pair off by sex. Stay with your partner and allow others to witness the bond that you are enjoying. When the two of you share meditation and prayer time, devote energy to the couples that you would like to experience a blessing. There are many other ways of inviting other couples into the joy that you share. Make a decision to do so and doors will open.

Prayer:

God, show us how to keep the doors of our relationship open to those who need a model of your love.

Let the Relationship Be of Service

To the Fellowship

Challenge:

The 12 Step communities draw strength from strong couples. Your bond can provide strength to others. If your relationship is an example of your God's love then you will want to share it with others. There are many forms of service that your relationship can provide if you and your mate are willing to make sacrifices. It can be difficult for recovering folks to relocate to a new geographic area and build a social group of recovering friends. The holidays can be particularly difficult for recovering people to cope with. Some will want an escape from the memories of past holidays. Others will be looking for activities that will provide them with the opportunities to create new memories. The sacrifices will cause you little actual discomfort save the act of including others in your thoughts and plans.

Reflection:

The bond that the two of you are building can bring security and a sense of belonging to others if you are willing to share it. Many individuals, couples, and families struggle with the need for fellowship. You and your partner can create opportunities for those who are searching to find a place to belong. You can open your home as a "dinner meeting" place or organize a recovery campout or trip to the beach. The opportunities are limitless when the two of you decide to focus on the greater good.

Prayer:

God, help me to look beyond our own creature comforts to the needs of those who are wandering.

Let the Relationship Be of Service

Our Family

Challenge:

We will generally have the most difficult time being an effective model of recovery and our Higher Power's love with those we are the closest with. The members of our immediate and extended families are likely to have been impacted the most by the stressful times in our relationship. If our children witnessed our emotional or physical struggles, they may have been deeply scarred. The members of our extended family might have lent a helping hand to us only to find us withdrawn and ungrateful. A romantic relationship can create chaos for the lives of those it touches and none more so than our primary and extended families.

Reflection:

If you and your mate have done the necessary "housecleaning" involved in Steps 4 through 9 with the members of your family, you have already gone to exemplary measures to amend the wrongs that you may have caused individually. The next step will be to take a look at the way that the "relationship" may have hurt others. If there are additional 9th Step actions to take, get to it. If the two of you believe that the work you have done individually has addressed these problems, then focus on bringing the picture of the changed romance to those you love the most. Let your children see the bond of communication and honesty that the two of you are building. Extended family members can be invited into the life you are building for each other through planned activities and joint works of service.

Prayer:

God, help us to find ways of serving those we have impacted the most. Help us to show them your love for us.

Let the Relationship Be of Service

To God

Challenge:

It is easy to become self-absorbed in the demands and desires present in our romantic relationship. We all have many demands including jobs to maintain, fellowship relationships to support, and family tasks to complete. If there are children in your life, you will have the extra responsibilities that accompany the blessing of parenthood. We have learned to balance the demands on our time and have found ways to be of individual service to our respective Higher Power; but little energy was spent using our romantic relationship to be of service to God, who we had been trying to keep in the center of our relationship. We had learned the meaning of the recovery adage that you can't keep it unless you give it away, but did not look to see how that applied to our relationship.

Reflection:

Prayer and meditation are excellent tools for keeping your relationship spiritually focused. You can begin to see God's love working in the relationship as you begin to handle communication and intimacy problems that created many arguments in the past. The flow of God's power in your relationship must be shared with others for the relationship to continue to flourish. Initially, we found ourselves feeling and behaving quite selfishly. We were afraid to expose our newfound closeness to the pervasive negativity of the world. Despite our fear, we decided to extend ourselves to other couples in social and fellowship settings. Much to our surprise, our emotional and spiritual security was not threatened or diminished. We were exhilarated by the experience and were replenished quickly from service to other couples and their families.

Ask for opportunities to be of service to your Higher Power and buckle up, for they will come.

Prayer:

God, help me to show the light you have given us to others. It is of little value if we keep it hidden and to ourselves.

Let the Relationship Be of Service

Weekend Workshop

We have learned that our union is strengthened when we decide to share our gifts with others. The time we have spent with other recovering couples has left us more grateful for each other and inspired us to continue working on problematic issues as they arise. Your relationship is a gift that you must share with others or it will lose its luster. We pray that you let it "shine."

John & Elaine

My Gifts to the Partnership

Reflect on the people in your life that could benefit from spending time with your relationship. If you have not been giving freely of your relationship, what do you suspect the obstacles are? Share your insights with a member of your support group. Make a list of the gifts that you believe your relationship has to offer others.

Make a plan to have your relationship be of service to others and propose it to your partner. Make sure you do not make commitments until you have talked about it with your partner.

Let the Slogans Guide You- Part 3

Easy Does It

Challenge:

Many of us are attempting to rebuild shattered relationships. Others of us have found a "new love" that we hope is the "right one." Whatever our situation, we find ourselves so pressured to make changes that we try and force "things" to happen before our God's time and the outcome is negative. Trust is compromised and support is withdrawn.

Reflection:

When your efforts to "make it happen" produce undesired results like fear, anger, and confusion, it can be helpful to focus on one of our timeless spiritual truths: "Easy Does It." Slow down and savor each moment that you have together. The past wounds will heal with patient attention and the practice of the Steps. The future plans will come if we live them today.

Prayer:

God, help us to slow down and use the gift that you have given us in the slogan "Easy Does It."

Let the Slogans Guide You- Part 3

Progress Not Perfection

Challenge:

Our desire for happiness and love can be so overpowering that we believe we can only feel secure in our partner's commitment when it is done with perfection. An expectation that our partner will never disappoint us or emotionally run from commitment raises impossible goals. Perfect commitments are nearly impossible and the expectation will cause unnecessary pain.

Reflection:

Focusing our sights on progress rather than perfection will relieve the pressure we are feeling because our spirit will not be depleted by hyper-vigilance. Focusing on perfection will cause us to see only failure. The only perfect commitment is the one our Higher Power made to us. All other commitments will fall short of perfection.

Prayer:

God, help us see the progress we have made with the same clarity that we can see the areas that need change.

Let the Slogans Guide You- Part 3

Expect a Miracle

Challenge:

The failures of our past relationships coupled with the painful memories of the marriages we witnessed as children can leave us feeling hopeless. Some of us grew up believing that marital love diminishes with time into a "mature love" minus the excitement and passion. Others experienced such romantic sickness that we came into our adult lives being sure that marriage was a waste. Still others actively participated in the destruction of numerous romantic relationships that had inflicted pain on both partners as well as those around them. A belief in true marital love seemed foolish at best and dangerous at worst. What can be done?

Reflection:

Acknowledge that a God of your understanding loves you and that love is made almost tangible in our commitment of love to a life partner. It may be difficult at times to maintain the faith that this commitment requires because of setbacks, disapproval of others who criticize the relationship, and our own fear. Understand that setbacks are to be expected because there are no perfect commitments. Solicit input about your relationship only from those you trust and who appear to be working in a healthy romantic partnership themselves. Remember that fear is an emotional perception and not a tangible reality. It is OK to be afraid, as long as the two of you are falling forward.

Prayer:

God, show us the miracle of your love in our union as we seek in all that we do to be of service to others in your name.

Let the Slogans Guide You- Part 3

Keep It Simple

Challenge:

From time to time, we will all succumb to the temptation to over-analyze the behaviors of those we love. This analysis will cause a myriad of problems in a relationship when we try to impose our perceptions on the lives of others in the form of commands and manipulation. We attempt to force our will onto the life of our partner and they recoil. We are hurt, feel rejected, and decide to retaliate. The game goes on for longer than expected and real injury is inflicted. Sometimes it is injury that the relationship does not recover from.

Reflection:

Developing a fuller understanding of the function of and motivation for a particular behavior of our partner's can be a purposeful and useful undertaking when we are trying to serve our Higher Power in our relationship. When we are attempting to manipulate our partner into some formula for change that is designed to restore or increase our security, the outcome is usually undesirable. When we are attempting to help our partner see what they cannot see without our help, and we have their permission and our God's blessing, the outcome can be mutually rewarding. "Keep It Simple": do not offer input without permission from your Higher Power and your partner and do not continue if it is not welcomed.

Prayer:

God, help me to see where I can be of service rather than give direction. I want to shed light rather than knock down doors. Help me to say what I see (when it is wanted) with your voice and your patience.

Let the Slogans Guide You- Part 3

This Too Shall Pass

Challenge:

When we are in emotional pain, it is difficult to remember not being in pain and harder yet to envision the pain coming to an end. The pain of the moment, if left unattended, will wake up all the pains of the past. This awakening will make it difficult for us to imagine life without pain, since the past and the present have become joined. When we are in pain, it is difficult to imagine that we will get relief because humans do not tend to project positive outcomes, especially when there is so little understanding of the reason for the pain.

Reflection:

It once seemed that faith was an attribute that was reserved for members of religious orders because of their lifetime commitment to serving God. Today we are realizing that faith develops when we trust in God and those who love us to guide and support us through difficult times. We pass through a crisis and emerge from the other end of a painful experience with the faith that we are able to survive the next one. Faith appears to be a gift, but it is really our experience and a product of entrusting ourselves to God and our fellows.

Prayer:

God, help us to remember that you are always available. Point us toward those who would be your servants as they support us through difficult times. Let us never forget that "This Too Shall Pass."

Let the Slogans Guide You- Part 3

Weekend Workshop

We have found the slogans to be great snapshot reminders of the spiritual truths we have come to rely upon. During our 33 years of marriage, we have had numerous times when we were individually or collectively locked in a downward spiral of fault-finding in the other partner. The slogans we selected for this week's theme have served us well when we found ourselves too intensely involved to see what we were doing or what needed to change. While it is vital that we learned to take the relationship and our commitment seriously, it was not a good idea to take ourselves so seriously.

John & Elaine

My Gifts to the Partnership

Choose a slogan that you have not used much and reflect on how you might use it in your romantic relationship.

Identify one of the slogans presented during the week that you see your partner use effectively in his/her recovery. Share your thoughts with your partner.

Co-Parenting

Parents, Not Gods

Challenge:

We will know no greater challenge in life than serving the God of our understanding through parenthood. It can be painful to see the damage we may have inflicted on our children. It is painful when we are unable to insolate them from the realities of life's disappointments. It is painful when we strive to improve our relationship with them and it appears that we are destined to take two steps forward and one back. There is much to do in our parental relationships that will require great personal change and ongoing personal sacrifice. How do we insulate our children from our mistakes?

Reflection:

Parenting can be an exhausting responsibility and sometimes our sacrifices go unnoticed by those we want to appreciate us. There may have been great injury inflicted in the course of the progression of our illness, but all wounds can heal if we are willing to attend to them rather than ignore them, as is so often the case. We have made and will continue to make mistakes, but Steps 4 through 9 afford us the opportunity to be an ongoing source of inspiration and motivation to our children if we practice these principles in all our affairs. Most importantly, we must remember that our children have a Higher Power too. Contrary to some of our perceptions of omnipotence, it is not us; we cannot be our children's God. If you have not parented children but have the opportunity to provide parental guidance to our youth, we hope that you will accept the opportunity.

Prayer:

God, help us to remember that we are striving to conduct ourselves in a way that is in keeping with your will for us. We have no ultimate authority over our children and any attempt to exercise such an authority will be met with rebellion.

Co-Parenting

We Are a Team of Two, Not a Mind of One

Challenge:

Many of us grew up in a generation that was lead to believe that it was paramount to present your children with a united front. Parents were discouraged from disagreeing with each other when presenting their views to their children. The model was one of unity and single mindedness, regardless of whether or not we viewed our parenting partner's behavior as inappropriate. If we are trying to be "of one mind" in our presentation to our children and one of us is troubled, then our presentation is going to be troubled and our guidance anything but sound.

Reflection:

Can we commit our shared emotional and spiritual resources to the task of raising our children? Can each of us commit to assuming 100% of the responsibility for raising our children (we realize that is 200% but one of us was never very good at math)? The math may be off, but the model underlying the 200% promotes the sharing of roles and duties. Fathers cannot "baby sit" their children, it is called parenting. Mothers do not have the market on love, as "mother's love" is not likely to be viewed differently by your God than a father's love. If our children can experience us as a team, they will have the benefit of both of our sets of experience, strength, and hope. If the two of us present ourselves as one mind, that makes each of us a half-wit.

Prayer:

God, help us to use our love and our commitment to teach our children about being on a team in life. Help us to teach them unity without loss of integrity and autonomy.

Co-Parenting

Powerless Does Not Equal Hopelessness

Challenge:

We often joke about the perception that we were powerless over our children after conception. It is a comical thought, but it is actually more true than not. We cannot control whether or not our children are born healthy. We cannot control when they will eat or be potty trained when we need it to happen. We cannot control the nightmares they have or the experiences in daylight that they might find frightening. We cannot prevent them from experiencing the pain of rejection or the disappointment of failure. We cannot control their feelings, their thoughts, how they permit others to treat them, or ultimately how they treat themselves. We have no power except to be models for living and examples of the principles of recovery put into action.

Reflection:

Powerlessness does not have to result in hopelessness unless we expect that we can prevent suffering. We can work diligently at our own recovery so our children can enjoy the fruit. We can work toward the elimination of our defects of character so we do not unintentionally cause others pain. We can amend our wrongs and prepare plans for change that are both spiritually and emotionally grounded. When we do these things, we will be rewarded with hope. Our children will ultimately benefit.

Prayer:

God, help us to be a channel for our children to know your perfect love and acceptance. Help us to know how to impart the values we have redeveloped in our recovery.

Co-Parenting

All Behaviors Have a Function

Challenge:

Our children have acquired rights that were denied to the generations before them. Many of us grew up understanding the implication of the rule that "children are to be seen and not heard." Some of us broke the rule as kids and suffered punishment and some kept the rule and suffered estrangement. There is no escaping the pain caused by a bad rule. Our children are now being encouraged to be seen and heard. But, at times, we do not like how they behave or what they say. We get hurt, take many things too personally, and become determined to control our children's behavior. The result will be painful for all.

Reflection:

All behavior has a function other than the common superficial explanations of attention-seeking, manipulation, and rebellion. We must learn to look beyond the obvious to both the internal as well as the external motivations for your child's behavior. They are not out to hurt you or cause you to die of a heart attack. They are looking for a way of expressing something that is painful that they do not fully understand. You can be a part of the problem and punish or you can be a part of the solution and investigate.

Prayer:

God, help us to look beyond the explanations that appear obvious and of little real value. Help us to avoid efforts at controlling our children in a way that could diminish their spirit.

Co-Parenting

We Must Be Our Child's Student

Challenge:

Many of us become overwhelmed from time to time with the task of teaching our children all that we are sure they must learn. All too often, our effort to bring the message home is hurtful and weakens our child's resolve for independence and autonomy. These are times of impatience and frustration, which are usually followed by rebellion and retaliation. Where are we going with the lesson? Can you really teach someone under such pressure?

Reflection:

It was once pointed out to us that there are two kinds of people in our fellowship. There are teachers and there are students. The teachers are those who repeatedly take back their will and attempt to control everyone and everything. The result is usually the same loss of control that is so painfully familiar to all of us. The students are those who are able to learn from the struggles of others. If we are willing to have our children teach us about what they need and what they are struggling with, we will grow in patience and tolerance. Our children will see us as wiser when we are willing to be their students.

Prayer:

God, help us to be a student in all we do and guard us against selecting who will teach us. We pray that we can learn from those who love us and those who fail to love us. We pray that the struggles of others will make us humble students.

Co-Parenting

We have learned so much from our children. Our reflection of meaningful lessons would fill volumes. The greatest gift, however painful it was to learn and accept, has been that we are powerless over our children. We joke with parents that reality has taught us that we were powerless over our children after conception. We can share, mold, model, encourage, and nurture, but our children have been endowed with the same free will that we have. There is no escaping the reality that our God has created us to have choice over whether or not we will serve him. We believe that if we were supposed to have protected them from the consequences of their choices, we would have been granted that power. We were not. We pray that you remember that your children were given freedom of choice.

John & Elaine

My Gifts to the Partnership

Examine a behavior of your child's that is disturbing to you and reflect on what purpose that behavior serves for your child other than defiance, resistance, attention seeking, power struggle, or parent abuse. We tend to assume the worst motive for our children's undesirable behavior and the best for our own. While reflecting on the above identified behavior, ask yourself how you might be contributing to your child's undesirable behavior. Do not be gentle with yourself.

Share with your partner what you admire in him/her with regard to their behavior with children.

Making Amends

Sorry Does Not Cut It

Challenge:

For many years, the medical profession viewed the alcoholic as a psychopathic deviant who was hopeless and incapable of change. The position was generally believed to be true because the alcoholic patient seemed to learn nothing from his/her mistake and appeared to be void of the guilt and shame sufficient for lasting change. While it might be true that many of us struggle to learn from our own past, the situation is far from hopeless or you would not be reading this meditation right now. Many of us have had guilt – tons of it. But most of us found that guilt, shame, or remorse were poor motivators for true change. We perfected countless ways of saying and acting "sorry." The end was always the same. We would return to the behavior that would injure those we loved. We needed to learn to do more than cry "I Am Sorry"!

Reflection:

There is more to do than acknowledge that we are sorry. Many of us had become quite familiar with our periods of deep regret. And although they were genuine, those moments were fleeting. Sorry would flow off our tongue like water off of a duck's behind. We would need to sincerely and diligently begin to examine the reasons for the behavior that caused the pain. A promise without insight into what must change will promote mistrust. Insight however, would be insufficient without a plan that was committed to that which could be measured. We should not be discouraged about the work ahead for the willingness will sustain us.

Prayer:

God, help us to look beyond the "sorrys" for the defects that we must bring to you. You know our hearts. You know that our regrets are real. Help us to see what must be changed.

Making Amends

An Amends that Heals

Challenge:

Mending an injured relationship requires a committed effort at developing the type of self-honesty and disclosure that enables others to see that the desire to change we have adopted is real. If your partner does not see the nature of your wrongs through your eyes, trust will be slow in the development. Whether the injuries have been repeated in this relationship or are reminders of past hurts, your partner is likely to be threatened by thoughts of "here we go again" and feelings of suspicion. Your task is to do more than point out your wrongs—you must be willing to change.

Reflection:

In our Step work, we are looking to heal our troubled body, mind, and spirit. The 8th and 9th Steps bring the healing process that we have been engaged in to the lives we have touched. If you are going to make a difference in the patterns you have subjected your partner to, you will need to understand them yourself. It is difficult to look at a pattern of repeated offenses because it can leave one with a feeling like there has not been much change. Nevertheless, a decision to thoroughly examine our behaviors and the defects of character that generate them will be personally freeing and promote a sense of security for our partner. People will begin to see that we are seriously making changes and healing will be the by-product.

Prayer:

God, help me to examine my defects of character so I can better plan for the behaviors that I must eliminate. I want to be free of the merry-go-round that continually returns me to the types of behaviors that injure those I love. Reveal to me those parts that will need to be removed. I will accept whatever support I need from others to resist the temptation of repeating the pattern.

Making Amends

Understanding Our Defects

Challenge:

It is common for our daily inventories or annual 4th Steps to contain the same wrongs time after time. For many of us, the repeat wrongs are a product of the defects in our character that we have failed to address. When our behavior continues to injure our partner the relationship will become prone to "heart attacks" which will eventually kill it.

Reflection:

While it is true that romantic relationships are like fertilizer for our defects of character, it is not true that the relationship's fate is sealed. The presence of defects of character does not ensure incompatibility. If we examine them closely, we can understand their origin and triggers that awaken them. Once patterns are identified, plans for change can be developed which will result in amends that can heal.

Prayer:

God, show me the truth about myself so I can present my shortcomings to you as an offering and commitment to change.

Making Amends

Planning for Change

Challenge:

Our partner will eventually grow tired of our promises to change when they begin to suspect that we do not know how to achieve a change. We may have shared with them the insights we have gained into our troubling patterns of hurtful behaviors, but insight without a plan for change will result in little change. If we are requesting forgiveness, there must be a plan.

Reflection:

After many years of study, we have concluded that the only way to change is to change. We must understand our defects and their common manifestations. Once their identities are clearly revealed, we can identify the ways that we are still deriving benefit from the defects. The benefits will have to be surrendered to God in a plan that replaces old coping strategies with new. These new strategies will promote the use of the Steps in all our affairs. The freedom found in this way will result in the need for far fewer amends.

Prayer:

God, prepare me for the changes that lie ahead. You know the dependency that I have developed on these ruinous behaviors. You know the lure they hold. You know my desire to be free of the gerbil wheel. Show me the way.

Making Amends

Granting Forgiveness

Challenge:

The repeated injuries we have endured have inflicted great pain, pain which has lingered long after the surface wounds have healed. We find ourselves wanting desperately to trust in our partner's commitment to change, but we are afraid. At times it seems the trust will never come. We are willing to forgive, but "never forget." The pain continues, but the cause lives within us, not our partner.

Reflection:

Perhaps it is not our responsibility to forgive the wrongs of another, as we are not God. We need to decide whether or not the insights offered seem genuine and the plan for change makes sense. To truly accept our partner's amends, we must be willing to participate in the solution. We can take an active role as a member of our partner's support group, in the process of monitoring the defect's triggers, and loving our partner through the painful separation from them.

Prayer:

God: help me to be a part of the solution, because my focus on the problem is killing me.

Making Amends

We can both remember when we used the words "I'm sorry" with little thought for the wrongs we had committed toward the other. It seems like we were always apologizing during the early years of our relationship. It might be said that the plethora of apologies were needed to compensate for our immaturity, but the harsher reality was that we worked our "program" better with strangers than we did with each other. The double standard we applied to our romance was finally addressed in depth when we began to work on the 6th and 7th Steps in our romantic lives. We hope that this week's meditations have inspired you to take a closer look at your defects of character, especially as they manifest themselves in your romantic relationship.

John & Elaine

My Gifts to the Partnership

Reflect on the defect in your character that has had the greatest impact on your romantic life and share your insights with a member of your support group. If your awareness becomes particularly disturbing, do not hesitate to seek professional help.

Examine your partner's positive progress in working the 7th Step and share your perception of where he/she has shown the most improvement. Ask your partner's permission to share your admiration with him/her.

Defects of Character Can Be Compatible

The Prospective Partners

Challenge:

The old adage that "opposites attract" has been bantered around for years. Its supporters subscribe to the notion that people attract like the opposite sides of a magnet. We offer no comments on the value of such a caution to prospective romantic partners because we do not understand what the phrase means. It is confusing to imagine how oppositeness between partners can create a bond. We are further confounded when asked to suggest positive interventions when the relationship becomes conflicted. If it were really the oppositeness that binds the couple, then logically resolving conflicts and illuminating oppositeness would cause the partners to repel from each other because it is the "opposites" that they are supposedly attracted to.

Reflection:

The attraction between perspective partners would appear to be identifications rather than differences. We have found that the partner's common suffering or injuries has been the greatest source of attraction. Often, the source of suffering each partner has experienced has given rise to the development of defects of character which may appear opposite, but in fact are quite compatible. We must look closely at potential hazards as well as the blessings.

Prayer:

God, help me to know my partner in an intimate way so I may better understand the experiences that have shaped his/her perception of the world.

Defects of Character Can Be Compatible

Physical Obstacles

Challenge:

Painful or dramatic life experiences that caused physical pain or sufferings in childhood are likely to be remembered long into adult life. The memory of those experiences is often awakened by intimate encounters with romantic partners later in life. The wake up call can be quite disturbing for all involved because the sufferer can react to the triggers as if they represent a clear and present danger. The reactions are often misunderstood to be themselves acts of aggression.

Reflection:

It is not uncommon to stumble over an emotional "trip wire" which sends your partner's ghosts running from the closets. Accidental triggers can be avoided when we adopt the practice of asking your partner's permission to initiate physically or emotionally intimate contact. Permission should not be presumed to exist because of past familiarity. Be careful, loving and respectful.

Prayer:

God, help me understand that my partner has a past that involves both affirming and traumatic events. Help me to remember the importance of keeping you in the center of our relationship.

Defects of Character Can Be Compatible

Emotional Obstacles

Challenge:

Early life experiences may have subjected our partner to grave emotional or mental distress. The injuries experienced during these periods may have left emotional scars, which left your partner more susceptible to having anxious reactions to unpredictable or ambiguous feeling experiences later in life. When your partner's reaction to the situation at hand appears to be an overreaction, it is likely that an emotional scar has been reopened.

Reflection:

Please understand that your behavior, however unwittingly, can generate painful recollections for your partner. Your compassion, support, and sharing of personal identification at times of emotional upheaval can promote healing in your partner and prevent unnecessary retaliation in yourself.

Prayer:

God, show me how to be a part of a healing solution. Help me to remember that the world does not revolve around me and that the pains of another do not need to be made worse by my inaccurate personalization.

Defects of Character Can Be Compatible

Spiritual Obstacles

Challenge:

When a person cannot escape from oppressive or abusive personalities, the spiritual injuries can be overwhelming, diminish hope, and generate depression. These bouts of depression can result in a broken spirit that fears believing in anybody or anything. The inability to protect oneself from the control of another can leave the victim emotionally and spiritually impotent and with the belief that they must rely on others for their security and general sense of well-being. They can be difficult to reach spiritually and will struggle to remain present in a relationship.

Reflection:

A decision to remain present in a romance requires that we make an effort to understand our mate's feelings and make efforts to have him/her understand ours. These spiritual shadows can be resurrected, but their caregivers must first understand that their partners are not running from them. They are running to the safety they perceive to be found in isolation. Avoid all "blaming" of the victim for running in fear...Extend your strength, hope and faith. Patiently await their return.

Prayer:

God, help me to remain a beacon of safety to my partner when he/she feels threatened.

Defects of Character Can Be Compatible

Building a Bond

Challenge:

Bonds can be formed very quickly in a relationship. Our common suffering and a common interest in recovery and worldly pursuits will unite prospective partners. The bond will need a great deal of attention or the loose knitting will unravel. The common suffering, which once attracted the partners, can become a wellspring of conflict that nurtures mistrust and resentment.

Reflection:

A true bond will strengthen with mutual self - disclosure and trust in a power greater than our relationship. A belief that a relationship will be our source of strength will weaken the bond. Trusting our Higher Power's guidance and having a willingness to have our relationship serve others will strengthen it. If we share openly with each other and trust our Higher Power we will grow. If we put our faith and trust in the relationship rather than the spiritual principles we have been given the relationship with wither and possibly die.

Prayer:

God, keep our focus on your will for us as individuals and as a committed partnership.

Defects of Character Can Be Compatible

Weekend Workshop

Our early romantic attraction to each other was tied to our shared identification with childhood trauma. We felt secure in the belief that the other person knew how we had felt. It was a bond of identification and support that developed very rapidly and we felt blessed by our ability to communicate and share so intimately. All was bliss until we began to become aware that our "similar" life experiences were going to give rise to similar or, at least, compatible defects of character. We shared a common past but we had a great deal of work to do to develop a shared life in the present. Our individual and shared work on the 6th and 7th Steps allowed the miracle of recovery to heal our past and unite our present. We hope that you will continue on the journey that you have begun together.

John & Elaine

My Gifts to the Partnership

Reflect on what your partner knows about your 6th and 7th Step work. If he/she does not understand your defects of character the way that you do, ask yourself why that is? Share with a member of your support group a defect in your romantic character that you believe has been removed and how you feel about that.

Make a list of all the positive recovery changes that you have witnessed in your partner and share it with the God of your understanding in a prayerful moment. Share with your partner what defect in your character you believe still affects the romance in your partnership.

Clearing Away the Wreckage of the Past

Sorting the Baggage

Challenge:

Each of us has brought baggage from our past relationships and some of us are just now discovering the mess that we have created in the current one. Whatever the situation, the sorting process can be confusing at times. Feelings associated with past relationships will surface in our current partnership, making it difficult to resolve conflicts that erupt. If we have not made efforts to sort out our past failures, our current partnership will become fractured.

Reflection:

Steps 4 and 5 offer a framework for identifying the baggage we are likely to have carried into our current partnership. The inventory and confidential disclosure will enhance our ability to be honest with others and ourselves. We will see the burdens and blessings we bring to the partnership. In order to clear away the wreckage of our past, we must be able to identify it.

Prayer:

God, help me to sort out the emotional baggage I have been hauling around. I need to discard that which I cannot change and call on your power to change the things I seem to be lacking the ability to do on my own.

Clearing Away the Wreckage of the Past

Mistaken Identities

Challenge:

When our feeling memories awaken a pain from our past, it is easy to blame our current partner's behavior for the injury we are feeling again. The pain could have awakened because either the feeling or the behavior was similar to what we remember. If we are quick to blame others for our feelings, we are likely to mistakenly blame our current partner for the hurt we are feeling.

Reflection:

Even though "mistaken identities" are common, they are an unnecessary challenge to recovery. If we assume the spiritual position that we are responsible for the quality of our own lives, there is no reason to blame others for our own feelings. Secondly, conflicts arising out of "mistaken identities" can be minimized by asking our partner if he/she was intending to hurt us in the way that we feel it. If the answer is no, look in either the front or rear view mirrors.

Prayer:

God, help me to take responsibility for the physical, emotional, and spiritual quality of my own life. With acceptance of that responsibility I will find the "courage to change the things I can."

Clearing Away the Wreckage of the Past

4ᵗʰ and 5ᵗʰ Step Work

Challenge:

The gift of sobriety, like many gifts of the spirit, is not without responsibility. The complicated and emotionally laden experiences of our past lives will need to be sorted out. Failure to complete a thorough inventory and a full self-disclosure will make it difficult to build an honest and intimate romantic relationship. Our past will either imprison us or serve as a source of unfailing wisdom.

Reflection:

Our past will be a great teacher if we are willing to examine the patterns in our behavior as well as that of those who have injured us. With improved insight, we can recognize unproductive patterns and can make changes in our behaviors that will make us more attractive to our partners. What we learn about the motivations of those around us will guide us in our efforts to teach them how to trust us.

Prayer:

God, help me to see me more clearly. Reveal those parts that need to be removed. Help me to understand why people behave as they do. Show me how to teach others to treat me with the love you have for me.

Clearing Away the Wreckage of the Past

Shipwreck Survivors

Challenge:

Each of us has known peril in our lives. The danger came in many forms. At times we thought we would never swim free of the objects of our fear. We are grateful to have escaped with our body in one piece, but the trauma endured by our spirit has created a lasting memory that will be either an asset or a liability in our romantic life. These memories will be triggered by fear or uncertainty.

Reflection:

Whether our memories of the shipwreck we survived are harmful or useful depends on how we use them. If we avoid examining the similarities between past and present relationships, we will react rather than respond to the fear. If we use the fear as an alarm of impending danger, we will work toward solutions. If we start running, we may never stop.

Prayer:

God, help me to hear the alarm when it rings. I do not want to run at every bell or I will always be cleaning up after the storm rather than taking precaution.

Clearing Away the Wreckage of the Past

Finding a Purpose for the Pain

Challenge:

Throughout the ages we have made excuses for the abusive behavior of others in phrases like "but I know he really loves me" or "I cannot feel angry ... she is my mother and you only have one mother." These excuses do not serve to better understand the hurtful behavior we endured—they are excuses and nothing more. The pain is said to diminish with time for "time heals all wounds," but does it really? We think not.

Reflection:

We attempt to make excuses for the wrongs of others or spend wasted years blaming them for the impact they seem to be having on our present life. Neither strategies are healthy and serve only to further diminish our spirit. We are unknowingly trying to make sense out of what happened. But, we cannot make sense out of nonsense. We can, however, use our past to be of benefit to others. When we use it as a spiritual aid, it will have purpose to us.

Prayer:

God, help me to use the past for the healing power it holds for those I would care for today.

Clearing Away the Wreckage of the Past

Weekend Workshop

Time does not necessarily heal all wounds. In fact, that time spent ignoring past injuries can actually create new injuries. There was no escaping the fact that our past life experiences influenced for better and for worse our attraction to each other. We could do nothing to change the past chapters of our life, but there was plenty of time to change the way the story was going to end. We decided that our romantic and sexual pasts were going to be our teachers and we were going to be its students. If you try to ignore the wreckage of the past, it will eventually clutter up your entire life. If you sort it out piece by piece with someone you love and can trust, you can actually heal old wounds. We have been amazed at what two could do in tackling what we had individually failed at. Keep clearing!

John & Elaine

My Gifts to the Partnership

What past memory has the greatest negative impact on your current relationship? Share your insights with your sponsor and solicit input on how you can draw on your God's power to overcome the ghosts of your past.

Reflect on an element of "wreckage" or difficulty in your current romantic relationship that has been overcome. Share with your partner how you feel about the freedom.

Resolving Conflicts

Feelings Are Not Facts

Challenge:

Many of us are still quick to blame those around us for the quality of our lives. We blame others for our own actions when we proclaim, "he/she really knows how to push my buttons." We blame others when we say, "she hurt me" or "he made me feel rejected." These ideologies are difficult for us to change, as they have been embedded in our culture. But, change them we must or our feelings will be controlled by others. That will leave us waiting for others to make us happy.

Reflection:

The feelings that we experience throughout our lives can be both painful and joyful realities. When we are hurt the hurt is real. When we feel loved we imagine it to be never-ending. Our feelings are real and do not need explanation or validation. When we begin to explain the cause of the feeling as being attributed to some event or person, we begin to view them as facts which must be proven. Take responsibility for what you feel. Keep in mind that others can not push your buttons because all the controls are internal.

Prayer:

God, help me to be who I am and feel what I feel without explanation, blame, or shame. Help me to remember that I am not what I feel.

Resolving Conflicts

Staying in the Moment

Challenge:

When conflicts arise in a romantic partnership, most of us find it hard to stay in the moment. It can be difficult to hear what our partner is saying when we begin drifting into the past or wandering into the future for clarification or defense. Avoid words like "always" and "never." Both are clear indications that you are looking to past experiences to fortify your perception of what is right.

Reflection:

If you are angry, talk about it without drawing upon past perceived injustices. Pulling out your partner's skeletons or your own will not strengthen your position. "I told you so's" do not improve communication, they kill it. You might very well be right but it will be for all the wrong reasons.

Prayer:

God, help me to remain focused when my partner and I are in conflict. If I run to the past or project into the future I will loose sight of your will for me.

Resolving Conflicts

Switching Sides

Challenge:

It is tough to be quiet when we believe that we are right. We make a great deal of noise to try and drive our point of view home. We can become mean, egotistical, and vindictive in our pursuit of justice. But in the end, our day in court has only created more suffering. Why is that?

Reflection:

Romantic conflicts produce no winners. If you win, the person you love loses and vice versa. Who do you know that openly chooses to be in a relationship with a loser? If you can not argue your partner's position, then you probably do not fully understand it. If you do not fully understand their position, how can you be sure that you disagree? If you stop to empathize with the picture your partner sees, the conflict will loosen its grip and you will be a better partner.

Prayer:

God, help me to be still and to listen without interrupting for your wisdom. It is present in every circumstance, including arguments we might lose.

Resolving Conflicts

All Conflict Has a Function

Challenge:

When romantic partners are engaged in conflict, certain themes begin to repeat themselves. The most recurring themes revolve around sex, money and parenting. While it is true that these areas can generate a great deal of disagreement, it is unlikely that they are always the problem. The dialogues appear to be a product of well-rehearsed scripts that the actors have committed to memory. Are these always the source of our problems, or are they symptoms?

Reflection:

It is difficult to call a halt to the drama when we are engaged in a conflict but when we do, the rewards are worth it. The next time you are delivering an academy award-winning performance, stop the action. Ask yourself what the purpose of our behavior is? Is this argument serving an ulterior function that we do not have the courage to disclose legitimately?

Prayer:

God, help me to be real with my partner. Circular arguments are unproductive and serve only to drive us further apart and further away from the knowledge of your will for us.

Resolving Conflicts

Conflict as Our Mediator

Challenge:

Conflicts that arise repeatedly around the same issues are never getting resolved initially, thus the circularity. We are addressing only the surface issues and not the core. When we are engaged in the repeated conflict, we are impressed only with the argument that we are making. When we are arguing our points of concern, we are unable to see ways of compromise and the responsibility of being of service is out of the question. We might benefit from meditation, but it is hard to find in times of conflict.

Reflection:

In the heat of the conflict, drop to your knees. That's right. Crazy as it seems you will immediately find power in your humble posture and the road to a "middle ground" will begin to materialize. You can trust that your Higher Power will begin to introduce meditation strategies as soon as he has a student.

Prayer:

God, help me to understand the benefit of placing myself in a position to hear your word. I am a slow, but willing, student.

Resolving Conflicts

Every romantic relationship has conflict, but that fact, in and of itself, is not a reason to minimize the presence of conflict in your romance. If we accept conflict as the usual and customary charge for romance or companionship, we are going to miss out on a great deal. We always reintroduced conflicts that one or the other of us believed to be unresolved. We have never been satisfied with the "eye for an eye" justice that prevailed in many of our prior relationships. We wanted to experience the love of a living God in our union and knew that we could not be satisfied with an "OK" relationship. We wanted fireworks, balloons, and to be skyrocketed to a fifth dimension in our romance. We pray that you do not get too casual or bored with each other.

John & Elaine

My Gifts to the Partnership

Make a list of the conflicts that you have experienced in your current romantic relationship and identify those that have not been adequately resolved. Look at the resolution from both you and your partner's perspective.

Reflect on the fears that you have about having those issues resurface and share them with your support group.

Talk to your partner about a conflict that you have had with another person in your life that you have yet to resolve and what impact the memories or the outcome of the conflict is still having on your life.

Coping with Jealousy

Squealing on Ourselves

Challenge:

Jealousy will give rise to a wide variety of hurtful behaviors. When it strikes, we will usually begin searching our memory banks for evidence from the past to support our current suspicion. If our partner has behaved poorly in the past, our "feeling memories" for those instances will be activated and we will be "assured" that our perception of what is going on now is accurate. Likewise, if other romantic partners have hurt us in similar ways, we will remember the feelings from those incidents and the memories will intensify our current situation. This is because jealousy, when kept silent, will wake up fear, sadness, projection, and insecurity. Once awakened, those feelings will quickly target our partner as the guilty party and the distance between us will grow.

Reflection:

Jealousy will feed off of past hurts and future fears, but its greatest source of nutrition comes from silence. If you want to break free of the grip of jealousy, begin squealing on yourself. Share your feelings with those in your support group and then to your partner, without blaming others for what you are experiencing.

Prayer:

God, help me to disclose the symptom of jealousy when it appears so that I can discover its roots.

Coping with Jealousy

Remaining Present

Challenge:

Jealousy can be consuming if we drift from the present to the past. The past may hold many examples of times when we misjudged others to be trustworthy and were deeply hurt. Projections of what the future may hold are equally perilous. We look into the future with an eye for signs of unfaithfulness and, all too often, the rejection we fear has been precipitated by our unbearable insecurity. Simply put, if you are looking for a wrong, you will find it.

Reflection:

Stay in the present. The past holds no verification for what you are feeling. The future will never come, so projection often brings rejection. This moment is the only reality and the only truth we have. Besides, we cannot make someone remain faithful to us. Also, it is important to remember that no matter how eloquent or forcefully a romantic partner makes a point, neither partner can be the Higher Power of the relationship.

Prayer:

God, help me to trust in you and grow in my understanding of your will for me and my partnership.

Coping with Jealousy

Partnership Not Property

Challenge:

Jealousy often generates a desire to protect our romantic interest as if our relationship or partner was property. The idea that someone could be stolen from us is really an absurd concept. However, our generation is full of tragic tales of a man "stealing" another man's wife. Or a woman that "breaks up a married man's family." Mates cannot be stolen like horses. Partnerships can be neglected or aborted, but never stolen.

Reflection:

We must remember always that relationships do not abruptly or mysteriously end in affairs or infidelity. The idea that a romance could end after ten or fifteen years because the couple found that they were incompatible is ridiculous. The only way it takes ten years to identify incompatibility is when neither of the partners is being honest with themselves. An ill romance will always warn the partners long before it dies. You may have been hurt in the past by "lost love," but it should not have come as a surprise. You simply ignored the warnings. The phone was ringing and you chose not to answer it.

Prayer:

God, help me to heed the symptoms of an ailing romance.

Coping with Jealousy

Understanding Flirtation

Challenge:

So, what is the problem with harmless flirtation? "There is no harm in looking at the menu as long as I do not order!" The reality for many of us is that flirtation is anything but harmless. It causes great harm in a romantic relationship because your real-life partner will not be able to measure up to your fantasy mate. That's right; flirtation is serious business because it involves pretending that you are in a relationship with someone else. This is where the problem lies: we can only be in one relationship at a time. We cannot be working on a romance with one person and pretending to have a romance with another.

Reflection:

Flirtation must be understood if the partners in the relationship hope to overcome its effects. Flirtation springs from some form of unhappiness or lack of fulfillment that is either internal, external, or both. It is not going to go away by demanding that it stop. It can be an obstacle that creates many challenges, but it must be overcome if your romance is going to survive. Some people use flirtation like a painkiller to comfort themselves when they feel hurt or disappointed by their mate. Remember, flirtation is harmful whether you are initiating it or receiving it.

Prayer:

God, help me to remain focused on my chosen relationship. Help me to check my flights from reality before they result in flirtation.

Coping with Jealousy

Encouraging Moral Support

Challenge:

Jealousy is seen by some as the curse of all romance. It is assumed by some to be a usual and customary aspect of being "in love." It will erode the fabric of a partnership if left untreated. Some will manipulate jealousy in an attempt to secure their partner's affection. Others will view jealousy as a form of flattery because their insecurity will encourage their partner to view them as a "prized possession." Whether jealousy is viewed as an evil or a blessing matters little; if the partnership does not unite to confront it, all will be lost.

Reflection:

Jealousy is not a necessary component of a romantic relationship any more than relapse is a part of recovery. Jealousy does not add to the breadth or depth of a romantic union. The idea of promoting jealousy in a partner for the purpose of encouraging them to be more intimate is absurd. Jealousy is not an independent force. It has no power of its own. Its power is derived from the partner's reaction to it. It is a defect of character, nothing more. If the partners join their emotional and spiritual forces, jealousy can be eliminated and replaced by mutual support.

Prayer:

God, help me to see jealousy for the simple coping strategy that it is. Help me to express my feelings in a productive way that promotes improved communication and intimacy.

Coping with Jealousy

Weekend Workshop

In the early days of our relationship, you would have found one of us so seized with jealousy that he (oops, we were going to keep the identity a secret) tried to end the relationship when he discovered that his partner had loved someone before him. As crazy as it may sound, the insecurity underlying the jealousy was so intense that he could not trust love unless his partner had been an emotional virgin. It is funny today to remember the insanities of those early days, but we can assure you that there was nothing funny about it at the time. Feelings of jealously should be taken seriously because they are always covering up something else that will eventually undermine the relationship if it is not addressed. When we began to allow our partner to help us with those intense feelings of insecurity, the jealousy began to lose its hold. We pray that you practice relying on each other for support.

John & Elaine

My Gifts to the Partnership

Make a list of every time you have ever felt jealous in your relationship with your partner and share it with a member of your support group. If you are currently being haunted by jealousy, make sure you get whatever level of spiritual or professional help you might need.

Identify one positive quality that your partner possesses that you sometimes become jealous of and share it with your partner.

Who's Really in Control

Blaming

Challenge:

We tend, in romantic relationships, to be too easy on ourselves and too hard on our partners. We may be willing to acknowledge "overreactions" to our partner's actions. We may be willing to concede that we "allow him/her to push our buttons," but we seldom look for our own mistakes. Blaming amounts to a forced effort to have our partner assume responsibility for a perceived wrong. When we are "keeping score," we want our version of the "truth" to be recorded. If we are going to keep accurate records we will need to post the blame on someone, usually the other person.

Reflection:

When we hold others responsible for the quality of our own life (which includes our reactions), we place the relationship in a very fragile state. Other people are not responsible for what we think, feel, say or do. We must take responsibility for changing what is ours to change. Likewise, our partner must learn to address the flaws in his/her character or live with the consequences. We must leave the score keeping and the blaming that supports it to the God of our understanding.

Prayer:

God, help me to keep one eye on you and the other on myself. With your help, my view of who and what needs to change will grow clearer.

Who's Really in Control

Challenge:

Some of us are quick to blame ourselves for the behavior of others. The partner who is always blaming him/herself for the ills of the relationship is placing the relationship at great risk of failure. If only one person is wrong, only one person is expected to change. If only one person is going to change, the relationship is going to grow apart.

Reflection:

The person who is "always wrong" has placed himself or herself in the role of the scapegoat. The self-proclaimed scapegoat is generally afraid to confront a loved one and risk a conflict that would threaten his/her security in the relationship. When we make excuses for the wrongs of a loved one by blaming ourselves, we rob him/her of the opportunity to grow. A healthy romance is one in which the partners are growing together separately. Does your relationship promote individual growth?

Prayer:

God, help me to assume no authority for the fullness of my partner's life. Help me to assume full responsibility for the emptiness in my own.

Who's Really in Control

Surrendering All

Challenge:

The 3rd Step of *Alcoholics Anonymous* (1953, p. 59) reads: "We made a decision to turn our will and life over to the care of God as we understood Him...." Does the 3rd Step apply to the fate of our love life? We tend to behave differently in our 12 step meetings than we do in our bedrooms. We turn over those behaviors that we fear will lead us back to our addicted selves in our meetings, but in romance we try to control the outcome through the use of manipulation, deception and dishonesty. Aren't these the strategies we used in the "old days"? Do we really think we can do it the same old way and avoid the same old outcomes?

Reflection:

If we want this relationship to be different, then we need to behave differently. When we become so concerned with how the relationship is going to turn out, we fail to see parts of the similarities between this relationship and the ones that failed in the past. But there is more involved in learning from our past mistakes than being a good student of history. We can gain insights about how to change from examining the past, but we can only change in the present. When we have an opportunity to resort to the flawed patterns of our past and we choose a new way, we have changed.

Prayer:

God, help me to see what needs to change so I can change it. Help me not to be so afraid of the similarities that I fail to learn from them.

Who's Really in Control

Accepting What We Cannot Change

Challenge:

Many of us enter romantic relationships with a focus on the relationship's potential. Our desire for companionship drives us into a union with a partner whom we really do not know. As time passes, the flaws in our partner become more noticeable and bothersome. We set a reconstruction plan in motion to change those aspects of our partner that we find objectionable. The course is usually rocky and sometimes disastrous.

Reflection:

Were there really so many things that needed fixing? Were they flaws or differences? Personality differences can be difficult to adjust to so we often try to remove the differences between our partner and ourselves. We snip here and erase there and before we know it the differences are gone but so is our partner.

Prayer:

God, help me to accept what does not need changing. Our differences can become complimentary if we look for the good in those we love.

Who's Really in Control

Only One Higher Power

Challenge:

Sometimes, it is difficult to let go of our illusion of control in romance. We may want so desperately for this relationship to work out that we begin to "tinker" with things that are better left to one's Higher Power. We struggle with a perceived sense of personal power that proves to be pure fantasy. We imagine our partner to possess the ability to make us whole. We entrust the "relationship" with the responsibility for our happiness. In every scenario we are hurt or hurt others.

Reflection:

There can be only one Higher Power. That Power does not need to be supernatural, but it helps. Natural human powers are limited to the knowledge that has been accumulated from past experiences and can be heavily influenced by defects of character. We must seek a power over the relationship that is greater than the sum of our combined wisdom. Many of us have searched far and wide, when all we needed to do was to look up.

Prayer:

God, help me to let go of the illusion of control and to understand that our demonstration of love comes from you.

Who's Really in Control

We hope this week's theme has introduced you to an expanded view of the control issues that can undermine the romantic health of a relationship. We entered our relationship with a bent toward agnosticism and, unfortunately, found the god of our relationship. In case you missed it: we found the god of our relationship – not God in our relationship. We had been working with the assumption that our relationship was our higher power. We would eventually bring a God into the center of our union, but we first had to make room. Our lives were cluttered with expectations and rules for how our partner was to behave. When we brought our understanding of God into the center, we began to look like a team for the first time.

John & Elaine

My Gifts to the Partnership

Make a list of the ways that you have tried to control your partner over the years and share the details of it with a member of your support group.

Give up some aspect of control in your relationship and do not tell your partner about it. Share your plan with a member of your support group and ask them, not your partner, to monitor your progress.

Sexual Maturity

Taking Responsibility for Our Own Values

Challenge:

The way we behave as sexual beings will serve either to enhance or diminish the quality of our union. Each of us is led by values that were, in many cases, shaped by undesirable emotional experiences. We may have learned to use our sexuality as a weapon or a tool, but in either case, the injury we wrought came back on us. Our sexuality is a gift that we can cherish or a burden that will tamper our growth.

Reflection:

If we engage in sexual activity that is in harmony with our values then "making love" makes more love. When sexual activity is out of sync with our values, the result is confusion and discord. Do not hesitate to pray on such matters. The guidance you will receive can be freeing.

Prayer:

God, help me seek your will for me in all corners of my life. I will not be ashamed of my sexuality.

Sexual Maturity

The Origin of Our Values

Challenge:

It is important to understand the origin of the values that can guide our behavior. If our values are spiritual they will be encouraging and nurturing. When the internal motivation is based in shame and condemnation, it is more likely to have originated in a human desire to control or restrict our behavior and therefore not spiritual in nature. Are we following bad examples or failing to follow good ones?

Reflection:

Our sexual life can be shame-free if we understand the experiences that have shaped our desires. If our behavior is motivated by rebellion to overcome the will of others, we can learn to break the restrictive chains without hurting ourselves. If we have drifted from values that are nurturing and life enhancing, there is hope. We only need to surrender to the knowledge of our Higher Power's will for us and begin to draw on that power to carry it out.

Prayer:

God, show me how to be free of both my oppressors and my rebelliousness.

Sexual Maturity

Sexual Intimacy Follows Emotional Intimacy

Challenge:

When sexual intimacy precedes emotional intimacy, trouble can not be far behind. When a relationship is new and exciting, communication and bonding seem to come easily. It is easy to talk in the beginning because there is so much we want to learn about each other. What happens when the questions get harder and the answers seem less clear? Often new couples will progress into sexual intimacy to fill the void created by emotionally lean periods. When sex becomes the fix for what ails us emotionally or spiritually, the relationship is in danger.

Reflection:

If you try to patch a worn pair of pants, the hole will soon grow. The holes we encounter in building a lasting romantic relationship must be filled emotionally and spiritually rather than covered over. The growth we experience will cause the sexual aspects of our relationship to grow richer and stronger. When sex is the "treatment," the relationship may not survive the cure.

Prayer:

God, help me to view sexual intimacy as a gift from you that flows from emotional commitment and spiritual integrity.

Sexual Maturity

Taking Responsibility for Your Own Body

Challenge:

Men and women accumulate a great many gender role expectations that can generate a wide variety of problems in romantic relationships. No single performance area is more greatly impacted than sexual intimacy. When performance expectations are associated with the "role" of the man or the "duty" of the woman, both members of the partnership will experience rejection.

Reflection:

The importance of taking responsibility for our own sexual fulfillment is nearly as important as it is to take responsibility for our own feelings. Do not assume the responsibility for "pleasing" your partner. Instead share in the responsibility for generating pleasure. Do not assume that your partner should know how to "please" you, only that they will be willing to share a pleasure bond that is developing.

Prayer:

God, help me to take responsibility for only my own sexual fulfillment. Love is not a contest whose prize is an orgasm.

Sexual Maturity

Serving Your Partner

Challenge:

Being of service to your partner is a challenge from our Higher Power and, as such, should be life enhancing for both partners. It is easy to view emotional and spiritual service in God's eye when we are talking about the fulfillment of commitments or the completion of tasks. Why is it so difficult to imagine that he has a will for us as sexual beings? In the sexual arena, most of us struggle with the idea of a God who would support them in the bedroom the way they feel guided and encouraged in their role as a parent or a 12 step sponsor. Why would the design for living change in the bedroom?

Reflection:

Who we are when we are naked must be the same as who we are in other areas of our lives. We have committed to the practice of spiritual principles in all of our affairs. Pray together for guidance in the sexual aspect of your relationship and you will receive it. Declare the bedroom "off limits" to spiritual practices and you will be knowingly stepping from grace.

Prayer:

God, help me to seek your will in all that I do.

Sexual Maturity

Weekend Workshop

We entered our relationship knowing very little about our partner's sexuality and even less about our own. What a journey it was to discover sex as a sharing of love! The trip, however, was not always pleasurable because each of us had historical components to our individual sexuality that needed attention and healing. This healing would take a while. The need for attention became evident quite early. We are grateful for having had the opportunity to grow up with each other. We hope you will not settle for "average."

John & Elaine

My Gifts to the Partnership

Write about the fears that you have encountered in the sexual development of your relationship and share your insights with your sponsor.

Identify the situations that still cause you to feel fear and develop a plan to get help.

Make a list of the sexual aspects of your relationship that you are the most grateful for and share it with your partner.

Tolerance

False Tolerance

Challenge:

When we tolerate our partner "in spite" of whom they are instead of "because" of whom they are, we are practicing a false tolerance. We may see ourselves as tolerating the quirky or odd behavior of our partner when we "forgive" them for their irritating habits. When the tide changes and our partner becomes irritated with some behavior of ours, we quickly recall "harms" we have endured and we are quick to defend ourselves as the one who has known greater harm. We are often heard to reply with lines like, what about all the good that I do?

Reflection:

If we had been truly tolerant of our partner's habits, we would not have used them to fend off criticism. Our spiritual challenge is to love our partners because of who they are, not in spite of who they are. The product of this love is true tolerance.

Prayer:

God, help me to love as you do. You know who I have been and who I am and you love me because of what you know.

Tolerance

Whenever We Are Disturbed...

Challenge:

Oftentimes, we look outside ourselves for the cause of the disturbance that we are experiencing. The first place many of us look is at our romantic partner. Part of the reason for the misguided blame is related to the high expectations we hold for our mate. Another motivator stems from a seemingly inherent tendency to blame others for the quality of our lives. Regardless of the motivation for our misguided focus, efforts to discover an external cause for our internal disturbance serve only to deepen our unrest.

Reflection:

It is a spiritual axiom that whenever we are disturbed, no matter what the cause, there is something wrong with us. If you can accept this simple truth, it will spare you countless hours of pain and suffering. When you are disturbed, first look within yourself.

Prayer:

God, help me to see me as clearly as I believe I can see others.

Tolerance

Working with Limitations

Challenge:

Some of us once believed that true romantic happiness could not be enjoyed until we could find the one person who had each of the best qualities we admired in all of our other mates. Others of us, perhaps thicker and sicker than the rest, believed the solution could be found in maintaining multiple romantic relationships at the same time. The latter of the two personalities may appear to be the really ill one, but both approaches will lead to the same disastrous end.

Reflection:

There are no perfect mates, only perfect unions. If neither your mate nor your union appears to be perfect, remember that the purest gold will come from the hottest part of the fire. A decision to work with the perceived limitations of your relationship or in your partner will produce surprising results. Individual weaknesses will grow into shared strengths and limitations will emerge into opportunities for mutual growth.

Prayer:

God, help me to see the opportunities in the obstacles. I know that treasures await those with imagination and perseverance.

Tolerance

Celebrating Strengths

Challenge:

The act of focusing on your partner's limitations can become quite habit-forming. In addition to the hazard of distracting you from self-examination, the habit of "fault-finding" in others will lead to a distorted perception of who your partner is. If your focus is on your partner's faults, then that is what you will see. You will not see your partner's strengths or be able to enjoy them.

Reflection:

Your partner's strengths may be difficult to see when the relationship is in conflict. During times of conflict we tend to focus on the vulnerabilities of others. In order to focus on strengths, you must be willing to drop your defenses and become more vulnerable. It is infinitely more important to celebrate your partner's strengths during difficult times than it is to protect yourself. Look for strengths in what your partner chooses not to do or say. Look for strengths in what your partner has contributed to your life. Look for your partner's strengths in the strategies being employed to defend themselves from your control.

Prayer:

God, help me to see the strength in others. My focus on their shortcomings will pull me away from you.

Tolerance

Avoiding Over-Identification

Challenge:

The act of over-identification occurs when your emotional investment in your partner results in a loss of personal perspective. When we begin to take on our partner's hurts or injuries as if they were our own, our security becomes threatened; when we feel the need to protect our security, we are less tolerant of others. We may sound as if we are supporting our partner by attempting to validate their feelings, but we are really fighting for ourselves.

Reflection:

We think it to be impossible to experience true tolerance of others when we are preoccupied with our own past, present, or future. When we are identifying to the point that we end up in the hole with our partner, it may become difficult for either of us to get out.

Prayer:

God, help me to see and feel what my partner has experienced without having over-identification cause me to lose perspective.

Tolerance

This week we have invited you to examine the dynamics of tolerance. When either one of us is feeling intolerant of the other, it is generally coming from some weakness in ourselves. It is not my partner that is intolerable. It is some behavior of my partner's that is triggering the emotion of intolerance. The feeling of intolerance is within us. It is not caused by what my partner is or is not doing. When we found ourselves becoming impatient waiting for the other, the result was intolerance. If we later discovered that our partner was unavoidably delayed, the intolerance is generally replaced with understanding. We pray that you grant each other the tolerance you would a sick friend.

John & Elaine

My Gifts to the Partnership

Make a list of the behaviors that your partner has found intolerable. As you look over the list, identify those behaviors that you intentionally commit to irritate your partner. If you are like us, you could not find any. So, if you're not doing it to bother him/her, then he/she is not doing it to bother you.

Identify one behavior that your partner reacts to with impatience and change it as a gift to him/her. Discuss your plan with your partner.

Fear/Worry

Keeping Our Focus on the Moment

Challenge:

It is most difficult to stay in the moment when we become fearful. Unbridled fear will drain spiritual energy faster than any other emotional state. When we are afraid, something is occurring in the present that reminds us of some past, unpleasant experience. Our distant and recent past experiences have left emotional scars that will be awakened by a current event. Once an unpleasant experience from our past has been awakened, we have but a few moments to choose how we will use it.

Reflection:

Our past will be either a blessing or a curse. We will use it either as a tool for change or a projection of what is to come. Fear is always triggered by unpleasant past life experiences. We are never afraid that something really wonderful is going to happen. Whatever we are afraid of is not happening right now. It has happened before in the past and it may or may not happen again. We are not afraid of the "unknown." We are afraid that the past will repeat itself. Stay in the moment. What you are feeling is not a fact. What you are feeling is not proof of what is coming.

Prayer:

God, help me to remain centered in this present moment for right now. Although I may fear danger, I am safe.

Fear/Worry

Worry Is Not Love

Challenge:

Many of us grew up with the mistaken belief that worry is a symbol of love. We might worry because we have difficulty accepting the way life is. Our partner may be in real trouble (or trouble that we have imagined) and we realize that there is little we can do to improve the situation, and we worry because we "love" them.

Reflection:

Worry is not something we do. Worry is the active practice of not taking action. When we are faced with a situation that is outside of our control, we can become fearful and depressed or we can become active. We must work on staying active. It takes effort to maintain a depressed mood. It can be exhausting to remain focused on what the outcome might be, but we tell ourselves at least we are doing something. Worry is not an action as much as it is the result of not taking action. When fearful, look for what you can change in yourself or your situation.

Prayer:

God, help me to focus on change and not on outcome. I will always be deceived by the fear of what I cannot see. Teach me to love when I am afraid, instead of worrying in the name of love.

Fear/Worry

Fear of the Unknown and Other Lies

Challenge:

So often we are told by spiritually-minded people that their inability to take action is based on their fear of the unknown. We have come to accept the principle that there is a fear of the unknown as if it were a spiritual axiom. It is difficult to imagine that some unknown outcome could be so terrifying. Consider how many known outcomes we have endured in the past we already have to be afraid of.

Reflection:

When looking to catalogue fears into type or severity, one will find an unlimited supply of irrational choices in an examination of childhood. As children, we know and survive many fears. Children are afraid of monsters under the bed and rumors that they can break their mothers back by stepping on a crack. Children relate to all types of fears, but you never hear them talk about a fear of the "unknown." Perhaps that is because they do not have enough past experience to project what might happen when they open a door in life. The phrase is "fear of the unknown," but one must suspect that the author must have skeletons in a closet he/she is afraid of opening the door to.

Prayer:

God, help me to remain focused on what I know so that I can be free of fear from what I do not know. I know you love me. About that I can be sure.

Fear/Worry

Prayer and Meditation

Challenge:

Fear and worry can wreak emotional and spiritual havoc in a romantic relationship because partners can quickly become absorbed in the fears of their mate. When the absorption occurs, the relationship deteriorates into conflict. There are many reasons for the development of a resulting critical conflict, but the most important is that the partners in the relationship lose emotional and spiritual perspective. Without perspective, our mate's feelings and thoughts become ours and we lose the ability to be helpful. Perhaps we allow the deterioration to occur because we have come to count on a crisis to clear the air. It is not uncommon to have our desire to "kiss-and-make up" justify the crisis-based means we use to get there.

Reflection:

You can avoid the absorption by staying focused on maintaining your own emotional and spiritual well-being. At times when you have grounded yourself through prayer and meditation, you can offer it to your partner. First, be an example of what you do when you're afraid. Then look for opportunities to invite your partner to share in the use of these simple spiritual tools.

Prayer:

God, help me to lead by example and invite rather than manipulate.

Fear/Worry

Letting Go and Letting God Before We Have To

Challenge:

Worry, as we have discussed, is an unproductive and sometimes hazardous strategy for coping with fear. Our recovery has included many fearful moments, which we have risen above. In some cases our survival has caused us to actually thrive and grow stronger. It was difficult at the time to see the fearful experience as a temporary condition. We were certain that the discomfort would never lessen, but we were wrong. Fear beat us into submission or we reached up to our Higher Power through an act of surrender; no matter the tactic, we survived.

Reflection:

We may have endured great hardship in our romantic lives and if we are reading this, lived to love again. Some would say we needed all the pain to enjoy the freedom of a spiritually centered romance, but we think not. In fact, we are certain that we could have done nicely without many of those endurance contests. We did not need to endure the fear, only surrender. The choice was ours; unfortunately, we took a long time to discover that we could let go and let God before we were beaten into submission.

Prayer:

God, help me to see the path to surrender to avoid needless suffering.

Fear/Worry

We entered our relationship full of fear about both of our histories of running from romantic commitment. Each of our first five wedding anniversaries came as quite a surprise to us. Neither one of us suspected that we could remain faithful and both expected to be bored to death by the start of our second summer. Neither one of us had ever made it through two summers in a row in a monogamous relationship. During the past thirty-three years we have "run" in every way imaginable. We'll still run a good deal, but we do not worry about it because most of the time we run toward each other. When you want to run, sprint for your partner.

John & Elaine

My Gifts to the Partnership

Make a list of the fears that you experience in your relationship and share it with your significant other.

Go to the God of your understanding in prayer for direction on how to cope with the fears you've identified.

Solicit input from your partner about what fears he/she has overcome with the help of your relationship.

Ask your partner to join you in prayer when you are afraid.

Doing What Is Right for Us

Avoiding Advice-Givers

Challenge:

Advice to the "lovesick" has always been readily available, but lately it has become big business. In the current trend of reality dating, "love" contestants compete for prizes that include love, romance, and a trip to the Bahamas. When the winners are chosen they are immediately elevated to "expert" status and the show's host asks them to share their secrets for obtaining love and happiness with the viewing audience. Beware of advice-givers, whether they are friends, family members, or game show winners.

Reflection:

The majority of marriages end in divorce during the first four years. Many partners stay painfully lonely in marriages that are bound by legal, monetary or religious obligation. Before taking another's advice, look closely at the personal experiences that your advice-giver is drawing from. If the relationship that your advice-giver is currently in is unattractive, do you politely excuse yourself? If your advice-giver has not been forthcoming about his/her own romance, run like hell. What you do not know might hurt you. Not everyone giving advice are taking it themselves. If it is not good for them, then it probably won't be good for you.

Prayer:

God, reveal yourself to me in my romantic life so I may better know your will for me. Reveal your messengers to me so I may see living examples of your love.

Doing What Is Right for Us

Couple Power

Challenge:

Romantic relationships can be very hard work and, at times, feel very lonely. It can be challenging to work on the bond that the two of you desire. There are demands from many facets of life that make it difficult to establish "couple time" and develop your sense of "couple power." In the worst cases, there are relationships that support separate beds, separate vacations, separate bank accounts, and the ever-favorite "guys" or "girls night out." The bond you desire will require commitment, change, sacrifice, and a willingness to ignore those around you who promote separateness in marriage. In short, there will be many opportunities for building "couple power".

Reflection:

A decision to build "power" in your relationship will not reduce your autonomy, eliminate friendships, or compromise individual interests. If you look for opportunities to be a couple in everyday life, you will be more of a couple.

Prayer:

God, help me with my fear that "us" will eliminate "me."

Doing What Is Right for Us

Identify Vs. Compare

Challenge:

One great strategy for building "couple power" is to spend time in recreation or fellowship with other couples. Some will quickly argue that there are very few other healthy relationships out there to spend time with. While it might be true that there are more couples that appear to be "engaged-to-be-divorced" than look like they want what you want, look closer. If the couple looks like they are struggling to produce spiritual principles in their relationship, it could be promising.

Reflection:

There are no perfect relationships as there are no perfect people. If you attempt to identify with rather than compare yourselves to the prospective couple, you might find yourselves gaining great support. A decision to unite "recovering couples" together can generate the same healing power we find in our 12 Step rooms.

Prayer:

God, help me to see you at work in the relationships around me.

Doing What Is Right for Us

Be an Example of God's Love

Challenge:

It can be difficult to avoid running when the work of our relationship becomes difficult. We might know what we want our union to be, but there are numerous distractions and demands that take priority. When it becomes difficult to find the time to do all we need to do, it is easy to forget about the needs we have as a couple. When we put "us" last, those around us will suffer as well. We need something to maintain balance during the lean periods of our relationship.

Reflection:

When there is little time available to care for "us," the best use of that time will be invested in service to other couples. Most of us have already learned that the greatest insurance against relapse is a strong commitment to serving others. Look for opportunities to demonstrate love to other couples and your own bond will be strengthened.

Prayer:

God, help me to remember that all is possible when we set out to be of service to you and our fellow couples.

Doing What Is Right for Us

Sharing in the Knowledge of God's Will for Us

Challenge:

There is great reason to be cautious when we find ourselves believing that we can see God's will for others. The traps surrounding the act of "God-playing" are numerous and always harmful, even when our motives are the purest. Because of this, we have overcompensated and learned to avoid communicating even harmless perceptions of what a Higher Power might want from a loved one.

Reflection:

In our own romantic relationship, we share a responsibility for communicating to our partner our knowledge of God's will for us. The practice of sharing our perception of God's will for "us" can be worth the risk because it will release additional power into our relationship. If we begin the sharing with a prayer together, we are guarded against slipping into "God-playing". If your partner does not agree with what you share, let it go.

Prayer:

God, give me the courage to "witness to my relationship" when I feel you nudging me into action. Help me to remember that the knowledge of your will for "us" is just a perception until it is confirmed by my partner.

Doing What Is Right for Us

Weekend Workshop

The decision to do what is right for us is not as selfish as it might sound. Each relationship must decide on the principles and values that will guide the coupleship. We have often behaved differently than our extended family members and others wanted us to. We were building a life together and one day, we hoped, a family that would share their lives with us. The adventure we sought and the visions we followed often led us out of physical contact with those that sought our attention. We heard from many who cared for us that we were doing the wrong thing. We did not argue; we did what was right for us without trying to do harm to others. We pray that you follow your Higher Power wherever that leads.

John & Elaine

My Gifts to the Partnership

Examine your history to determine if your path has been designed to hurt others. If you find wrongs, amend them.

Make a list of the paths that you've followed that others have been disappointed with. Share your reflections with a member of your support group.

Share your reflections on your historical pathways with your partner.

Examine your future plans with your partner to be sure that the two of you are doing what is right for the relationship. Make a decision to do errands together rather than separately when you can. To do so would be practicing couple power in everyday life.

Roles Are Played By Actors

Being Vs. Acting

Challenge:

The partners in any romantic relationship have their individual strengths and weaknesses. One partner will bring skill to a task that the other is lacking in. One partner may be better situated emotionally or physically to assume a responsibility that is not well suited to the other partner. This flow of service of one to the other is very healthy. Danger comes when there is an expectation that one partner is to assume sole responsibility for a prescribed role or function based on gender, age, or experience. Roles are dangerous because they are rigid and confining.

Reflection:

If we can eliminate role expectations from our relationship we are going to know greater peace as a couple and more fulfillment as individuals. When we practice being who our God intends for us to be in this relationship, we will be encouraged to take risks and, as a result, grow. Being is a dynamic process while acting out a role is static and predictable.

Prayer:

God, help me to see who I can "be" in this relationship rather than how I should "act."

Roles Are Played By Actors

The Man of the House

Challenge:

Surrendering role expectations that were in many cases formed in our childhood can be a difficult task. Young boys are often shaped by expectations of both parents into becoming a "man." You or your partner may have received extensive training in the art of "being a man." "Men" can be trained to believe that certain behaviors are more appropriate for them than their female counterparts. Likewise, many will be taught to believe that females are more instinctual lovers and/or more nurturing parents. There are many such gender expectations that cause great harm to spiritual romances.

Reflection:

What we are to feel and how we are to act is not dictated by our gender. Boys will become men if they live long enough. A man is a grown up boy; nothing more or less. The way that a man behaves is not dictated by his gender, as gender carries no inherent benefit or limitation. Biological differences aside, men and women are the same. If we believe differently, we are going to cast our partner in a role he/she may be ill prepared for and we will both be hurt.

Prayer:

God, help me to receive my partner as a gift from you that needs to be "unwrapped" with love and care. Help me to avoid judging the contents by the "packaging."

Roles Are Played By Actors

The Little Woman

Challenge:

Women who join a romantic partnership need never be limited by gender role expectations, but many are. If you or your partner has been led to believe that women are from a different planet than men, it is little wonder that there has been misunderstanding and needless hurt. How a woman will behave cannot be predicted by the sole knowledge of her gender. We are not destined to be kind and gentle like we are destined to have blond hair and blue eyes. Many women have been lured into unhealthy relationships because they have been afraid to challenge the gender training they have received.

Reflection:

The biological differences between women and men are poor predictors of a partner's abilities or potential. When we view our partner through the glasses of gender prejudice, we will limit their ability to grow. When we continue to expect our contribution to be limited by our gender, we are likely misunderstanding the knowledge of our Higher Power's will for ourselves.

Prayer:

God, help me to see the opportunities for us to be united in our differences and as a source of strength for our partner to be all that she/he can be.

Roles Are Played By Actors

Helping Our Daughters Become Women

Challenge:

It is fairly easy to raise a daughter to adulthood who accepts the social and romantic restraints that women have suffered under for years. However, a female is not endowed at birth with special qualities that make her especially suited to any role in life different than a male other than child bearer. That being said, her gender should not prevent her from following any path she chooses and no one should expect her to assume a subordinate role to a male.

Reflection:

The responsibilities of participating in the raising of a daughter to womanhood are demanding and rewarding. We want to take special care never to promote adherence to "lady-like" behavior. What society expects of a "lady" may not be good for your daughter. We want to encourage her to dream, to risk, and to accept only the limitations she interprets to be her Higher Power's will for her. If we help her to learn interdependence without the loss of autonomy we are of great service to her.

Prayer:

God, help me to teach my daughter by example how she is to be treated. Help me to raise a daughter a son of mine would be blessed to marry.

Roles Are Played By Actors

Helping Our Sons Become Men

Challenge:

If we want our sons to develop into men we can be proud of, we must pay attention to what we show them. If we are heavy-handed in our discipline of them, we might teach them to be unnecessarily tough. If we discourage them from the display of their emotions, we may rob them of tenderness. If we are their mothers, they will watch us to learn how men should treat women. If we are their fathers, we will show them how women are to be viewed.

Reflection:

Great care should be taken in raising a boy to be a "man." We want to raise a son who is capable of full participation in a committed romantic relationship. We must teach him the language of feelings and how to perform courageous acts of tolerance and empathy. We must show him equality. But most of all, he should witness the benefit of keeping a power greater than himself in the center of his love relationships.

Prayer:

God, help me to raise a son into the type of man I would want a daughter of mine to marry.

Roles Are Played By Actors

Weekend Workshop

We entered our relationship with many ideas about how we were going to do it differently than the relationships we had observed growing up. We were not going to be locked into the stereotypical roles of the housekeeper or the breadwinner. What we had not planned on was the unpredictability of life's challenges, which forced each of us to assume responsibilities and roles we had not counted on. We took on tasks that we might not have but we did it for the greater good. We hope the two of you stay flexible and accept those tasks that are necessary for the relationship to thrive.

John & Elaine

My Gifts to the Partnership

Make a list of the adjustments to your original plan that you made for the greater good of the relationship. Feel good about the service you rendered.

Make a list of the changes that you still need to make and discuss it with your significant other.

Make a list of the changes that your partner has made for the relationship and extend your gratitude in some way.

Ask your partner to share his/her perception of one small change you could make that would contribute to the greater good of the relationship.

Self-Fulfilling Prophesies

It Was Never Going to Be This Way

Challenge:

Many of us had the gross misfortune of growing up in the shadow of a tumultuous and unloving marriage. We attempted to comfort ourselves late at night, when the fights were raging downstairs with the promises of the desperate: "I will never let a man/woman treat me that way" and "I'll never get married, you'll see." Who were we talking to back then? Our parents weren't listening. We suspect we were talking to ourselves.

Reflection:

Unfortunately, many of us were not really listening to our self-talk. It is understandable, though, because we were not really trying to keep ourselves out of future trouble. We were simply trying to numb the pain of the present. Many of those nights we promised and pledged and eventually we fell asleep. This went on night after night for months or years before we found ourselves awaking to a relationship that was just like all the others that did not work. When we woke up from our sleep, we were in a romantic relationship very much like the one we swore to avoid. The difference is, now we know it and knowledge can lead to freedom if we choose to change.

Prayer:

God, help me to act on what I see rather than hide from all the mirrors.

Self-Fulfilling Prophesies

But You Were Never Going to Hurt Me

Challenge:

Many of us have moved from one romantic relationship to another, thinking we are leaving pain and going to find love. We then enter a romance with expectations of love everlasting. We wanted an end to our loneliness but were cautious to find someone different from the others. Previous relationships may have been unpredictable and laced with hurt and rejection, but this one was going to be different. We would not hurt or be hurt in this one.

Reflection:

It is right and justified to end a relationship in which the partners cannot seem to stop hurting each other. However, it is deceptive to believe that a romance will be devoid of pain. Every deeply intimate relationship will know pain, as it is nearly impossible to grow without it. When two people move toward emotional and spiritual intimacy, they will get close enough to cause emotional injury. They will let each other down, fail to support one another at times of real need, and place expectations on their partner that only a Higher Power could fulfill. This is inevitable. Try not to run from every pain or you may never stop running. "Pain is the touchstone of all spiritual progress."

Prayer:

God, help me to stay where I am at until leaving is not the solution to the problem.

Self-Fulfilling Prophesies

I Can't Take It Much Longer

Challenge:

When we find the behavior of our romantic partner intolerable, it can be frightening. Most relationships encounter real problems that have the potential of causing irreparable damage to the union. When we encounter a problem that threatens the security of our relationship, we either take action or assume a position of inaction. When we become frozen in inactivity, we can be lured into the illusion that worry or empty ultimatums are actually going to help the problem. The use of empty ultimatums like "I Can't Take It Much Longer" is creating the self-perception that we are doing something to resolve the issue. In reality, this amounts to no more than a threat we are making to ourselves.

Reflection:

The ultimatums that we give ourselves seldom motivate us to change. They serve only to diminish our spirit. If you "can't take it anymore," it is because you do not know what to do next. When a situation appears intolerable, begin with prayer for the knowledge of God's will for you and the power to carry that out. Once you are spiritually focused, begin to get help for yourself rather than present the case against your partner. A decision to work on yourself will bring clarity to your situation.

Prayer:

God, help me to keep the focus on myself and grant me the courage to change the things I can.

Self-Fulfilling Prophesies

We Were Meant to Be Together

Challenge:

It can be difficult to know how to acquire the knowledge of our Higher Power's will for us as a romantic partnership, but it is always available. Many of us grew up with the idea that romantic magic should be self-sustaining. When the sparkle of the magic begins to dull, we can become frightened or confused about what our purpose is. As the magic disappears it is common for partners to wonder whether or not they are really "meant for each other."

Reflection:

Romantic magic is not self-sustaining. If we do not cultivate and nurture romance, it will die. Before the romance dies, we may be tempted toward flirtation with others. If our flirtations are reciprocated, a spark of magic will be ignited. The new spark further convinces some that the relationship they are in was not meant to be. Many of us ran from one relationship to the next looking for the never-dulling magic. Do not accept a bad relationship, but understand that the magic is created by lovers, not fate. If we decide in our minds that we are not meant to be together, it is inevitable we will not stay together for long. Be careful not to put words into your God's mouth when looking for guidance, especially when it involves romantic magic and outside flirtation.

Prayer:

God, help me to know and pursue the kind of exciting love you promised me.

Self-Fulfilling Prophesies

I Will Never Be Enough

Challenge:

A romantic relationship will involve many challenges. One of the commonly experienced challenges is finding the balance in which each partner is able to experience their own emotional security. A healthy romance will challenge the partners to develop a healthy spiritual foundation for individual security. If a partner's emotional security is tied to the stability of the relationship, there will be a great many problems. Our security needs to be trusted to a power greater than ourselves, not to a single person.

Reflection:

When we tie our security and well-being to the approval of a romantic partner, we will frequently disappoint both our partner and ourselves. The failure to find a spiritual basis to our security and self-esteem will cause us to feel like we never measure up. If it feels like you will "never be enough," then you are probably looking in the wrong place for recognition. If you decide you will never be enough, the negativity you deposit in the relationship may break its back.

Prayer:

God, help me to look to you to understand who I am to be.

Self-Fulfilling Prophesies

Weekend Workshop

If you want to avoid repeating the past, you will need to do more than make promises. Any promise that begins with "I will never be like..." is likely to end in regret. We frequently found ourselves so blinded by our fear of "...ending up like them," that we missed the signs that we were repeating the past. 12 Step groups occasionally undertake "group conscience" inventories to conduct a critical assessment of the group's strengths and weaknesses. It is a process that can be initially uncomfortable but the group is generally strengthened in the process. We have found that the best insurance against the marriage we were "trained" to have is to closely examine the one that we are in. We pray for your continued honesty with each other.

John & Elaine

My Gifts to the Partnership

Make a list of the behavior you wanted to make sure your relationship avoided.

Discuss with your partner those behaviors that you need work on.

Share with your partner one fear that you have for your relationship and focus on supporting each other.

Join your partner in prayer for the marriages of your childhood that are still in pain.

Marriage College

Knowing Your Professors

Challenge:

Our enrollment in "marriage college" begins at about six years old and continues on until our early teens. During that time we are, in a sense, videotaping the lectures that we will watch over and over for many years to come. Our professors are primarily the adult role models in our lives, although some lessons will be delivered by guest lecturers on T.V. and in movies. The experience will leave some of us swearing off marriage and others chanting, "I will never be like them."

Reflection:

Our "professors" are not necessarily evil people, but some of the lessons we experienced will seem like curses when we try to make our romantic lives different from what we have seen. It is important to remember that the faculty in "marriage college" is not trying to teach us. They are living their lives according to the training they had and the decisions they have made. Quite often, they do not realize others are watching, much less taking notes. We can learn a great deal from them if we can stop blaming them for who we have become. Instead of using their lectures as a guide for life, we can use them as something to learn from.

Prayer:

God, help me to understand that what I "learned" can be replaced with new material if I am willing to remain a student.

Marriage College

Drop/Add

Challenge:

Our "marriage college" experience may have created an unhealthy picture of romantic commitment for us to model, but we have choices as adults to challenge the lessons we have learned. Those lessons, no matter how bizarre, could not dispel the spiritual innocence we were blessed with as children. The scary and lonely times we faced may have forced us to grow up faster than perhaps we should have, but the faith in what is good about the God in us could not be removed. The challenges of childhood will leave us with a great deal to carry into adulthood. It will need to be sorted out.

Reflection:

The responsibility to sort out our past is a spiritual challenge each of us must face. All that we have learned is not trash to be discarded. At the same time, not everything that we were told was true. We have an opportunity in our relationship today to drop those lessons that we have found to be unproductive. The lessons we are learning through recovery about honesty, intimacy, and love can be added to our new program of studies from which we will never graduate.

Prayer:

God, help me to separate the junk from the gems. I blame no one for how I have lived and will look for opportunities to spread what I am learning about new ways of living to others.

Marriage College

Deciding on a Major

Challenge:

These days, college students change majors almost as often as we once changed relationships. In the past, when the work got difficult we "wisely" decided that we had foolishly rushed into a romance with the wrong person. There were many explanations for what was wrong with him or her, but little focus on how we have behaved. Many students choose majors because of how they imagine they will feel in the role the course of study is preparing them for. As so often is the case, the actual journey is much different than the imagined outcome. Many of us have difficulty seeing the truth and narrowing our romantic focus. We wander around looking for the "right one" or remain stuck in an empty relationship, waiting for our partner to show up.

Reflection:

We can avoid great hardship if we stop entering romantic relationships for the potential that we see in them. If we entered a relationship with an unspoken condition that the other person will be acceptable when they change into a particular image that you have, you are lying to yourself and to your partner. Instead, an in depth discussion of our core and applied values will help us to clarify what we believe in. If we do not share common core values, we will not progress to mutual happiness and fulfillment.

Prayer:

God, help me to declare what I believe in all that I do. Help me to keep my eyes open in every circumstance, including relationships. Help me to avoid the rose-colored glasses of potential. Instead, help me to focus on my values and what is important to me.

Marriage College

Developing Healthy Mentors

Challenge:

Finding new teachers can present a great challenge. We have unwittingly followed the teaching of individuals who, in reality, did not appear contented and fulfilled in their own relationships. We believed them when they proclaimed that we "made our bed and needed to lie in it." We reluctantly accepted the time-honored wisdom that said that mature relationships accept that the loss of excitement is to be expected and that, in time, a couple gets used to a relationship of convenience.

Reflection:

The partners in a relationship of convenience will drift apart if either one of them begins to grow. Contrary to popular belief, relationships without romantic and playful excitement will not learn to do without it. If excitement is nowhere to be found, the excitement that they seek will be generated by conflict. The curse that sentences people to lie and die in the "beds they have made" is a curse, not a spiritual axiom. If curses in fact exist, then they exist to be broken. Never settle for what others have told you will be. Bring a power greater than yourself into the center of your romance and buckle up.

Prayer:

God, help me to know the romantic love that you intended for me to enjoy. I am ready for the thrills and the spills.

Marriage College

A Spiritual Focus

Challenge:

From time to time, it is important to examine the focus that the relationship is pursuing. If we pursue things and power alone, our relationship will be defined by what we have and what we control. If the majority of our time as a couple is spent in the acquisition of power and prominence, then we are likely to be very lonely because other people will become objects. If we set out to have things and people serve us, we will grow weaker as a couple.

Reflection:

Our relationship must have a spiritual focus if it is going to be different than the other unsuccessful ones of our pasts. A decision to focus on our spiritual needs first will place us in a position to be of optimal service. There are an infinite number of ways to accomplish that end. The easiest is to look for opportunities to be of service to other couples. Are there other couples that could benefit from all that we have? What do we have to teach to others?

Prayer:

God, help me to keep my focus on the ways you have taught us to love.

Marriage College

Our presentations of the meditations associated with "marriage college" were not an attempt to post blame on anyone. The quality of our relationship was our responsibility. We would look to the past in order to better understand the strong hold that some defects of character had on us. The romances we studied as children left us afraid of ever living in a committed relationship. We got the retraining we needed to overcome the behaviors that became nearly automatic. We needed to return to school and hope that you will have the courage to do so if you need it.

John & Elaine

My Gifts to the Partnership

Identify the lesson you learned as a child about romance that has been the most difficult for you to replace with healthy behavior. Write a few paragraphs about what you discover and share it with a member of your support group.

Prepare a list of lesson topics you would want your children to learn if your relationship has/were to have children.

Carrying the Message

Knowing Your Story

Challenge:

We get into great trouble when we assume that our romantic partner knows what we are thinking and feeling. The times we have suffered past disappointment and rejection should be painful reminders to us that assumptions can be dangerous. The tendency to assume that our romantic partners should know our needs is often found in unhealthy relationships.

Reflection:

Most of us are familiar with the phrase, "if you loved me..." When you use the phrase it always assumes two things. First, your partner is assumed to know how it is that you want to be loved. And secondly it assumes that your partner knows how to love in the way you desire. Please remember that it is your assumption, not your desire that is dangerous. Many times partners in a relationship have expectations of what their partner should know and the partners have not told each other their respective stories. So much of what we expect and assume is tied to our past. The stories you tell will involve the life experiences that have helped to shape your values, coping strategies, and your goals for the future. The stories can be told through your expression of the joys and pains you have known as well as the successes and failures you have experienced. The topics are limitless and you do not have to worry about being able to prove anything. You are the only expert on the subject of you. Before the next fight over misplaced assumptions, tell your partner your story.

Prayer:

God, help me to remember that it is important for me to tell my story to those I would have love me. I know that the first person I must carry the message to is my partner.

Carrying the Message

Experience

Challenge

The message of hope, love and recovery, as we have discussed, must first be shared with our partner. We cannot however, rest there. A couple needs to share what they have learned with others if they are going to continue growing. The intimacy that develops within a romantic relationship is a beautiful thing of great spiritual value. It is common in the early periods of growth to want to pull away from others and protect what we have.

Reflection

Whatever we keep for ourselves will dry up and blow away. Whatever we share with others will multiply and create an inexhaustible supply. The experiences that you share with other couples will help reduce the fear and insecurity they might be experiencing. The story you share with other couples should include past and present challenges and joys so they can get the whole picture. The experience of telling your story to others will strengthen your bond and reduce the occurrence of senseless arguments.

Prayer

God, help me to tell the stories that will help others to be closer to each other and nearer to you.

Carrying the Message

Strength

Challenge

Relationships, as you know, can be a great deal of hard work. It is work that must be done while the rest of the world continues to spin. Unfortunately, life does not take a vacation while we work on building a romance. It may have been so when we were teens, but for most of us, life is pretty full these days. The experiences have been sharing with other couples have made a valuable contribution to their sense of well-being, but there is more you can do. When you share your strength with them, your 12 Step work can be more productive.

Reflection

The strength you share is likely to come in the form of deeds. An invitation to dinner at a fellowship meeting can demonstrate your commitment to another's relationship and could strengthen their commitment to each other. You will be repaid several times over. The acts of service like babysitting and helping out with life tasks can help to reduce the stress in another's relationship and bring some joy to your own.

Prayer

God, help me to find ways to extend our couple's strength to others.

Carrying the Message

Hope

Challenge

The challenges that accompany a romantic relationship can be quite frightening at times, especially when it seems that it is all work and no play. Couples, who are struggling to rebuild a relationship that was nearly dismantled by an addictive disorder, might have real difficulty maintaining hope. They will see many relationships around them that succumb to divorce, infidelity, and in some cases joint relapses. We have all learned that fear and hope can not exist in the same space, but hope does not descend on us just because we want it to.

Reflection

Hope seems to be what we acquire when we learn to trust the process of recovery. As we come through a difficult time, as a result of the utilization of spiritual tools we have available to us, we develop hope. Hope can develop when we witness "miracles" in the lives of those we know. When you accept the responsibility to carry the message of romantic hope to couples you meet, your courage and kindness will not go unnoticed.

Prayer

God, bring me opportunities to carry the message of hope to injured relationships.

Carrying the Message

Giving It Away to Keep It

Challenge

Carrying the message to other couples can stretch your patience and threaten your serenity. Many of the couples that you will share your experience, strength and hope with may declare that they are open, but behave defensively and sometimes even challenging. Some couples may try to take advantage of your kindness while appearing to be needy. At times, you may wonder why you are bothering to make sacrifices of time and talent for unresponsive or ungrateful people. Why not just lock the gate and get cozy with your partner? Who cares anyway?

Reflection

When your message is not well received, examine your presentation. If you have kept the focus on your own experience, strength, and hope, and you have avoided advice and criticism, then move on to the next opportunity. Many who will desire what you have won't want to do what you have done. Remember that the message that you are carrying does not have to be received fully or acted upon. It just needs to be delivered in a way that reminds you of your romantic fortune and the grace with which you earned it.

Prayer

God, help me to avoid score keeping as I go out to do your bidding. Introduce me to those who are interested in your gift of romantic love.

Carrying the Message

The importance of sharing the experience, strength, and hope that your partnership has acquired cannot be over-emphasized. Every part of your relationship that you decide to share with others will be strengthened in the process. We encourage you to make the tithing of your time in service to other couples a critical part of your spiritual "gift-giving." We pray that others will join you in your romantic journey as a result of your sacrifices.

John & Elaine

My Gifts to the Partnership

Identify a couple that you can be of service to this week and imagine what it would feel like to be them receiving your service.

Share your reflections on the above task with someone that loves you.

Work side by side to craft a list of those aspects of your relationship that the two of you are the most grateful for and share the list with another couple.

In All of Our Affairs

Being Committed

Challenge:

The fear of commitment surely ranks among the topmost frequent explanations for the breakup of a romantic relationship. Some will argue that the hesitation that many have to make a commitment to a romance is related to poor romantic matches. Others will claim that fear of commitment is rooted in unresolved trauma. Whatever the individual cause may be for the failure to make a romantic commitment, the reluctant partner is headed for a pattern of long, lonely walks in the desert in search of true companionship and love.

Reflection:

True companionship and enduring love flow from commitment, not to it. Chances are that those who repeatedly resist romantic commitment also evade commitment in many areas of their lives. We can and should plan and have goals in our lives, but they should remain flexible to allow for our God's will for us to make us more adaptive. The knowledge of God's will for us is always received in the present moment. If we remain in the moment, then commitment will hold no fear. When we run, constantly looking for the perfect "soul mate," we will miss the opportunity to participate in the creation of one. The union of two souls forms a soul mate.

Prayer:

God, help me to remain in the moment.

In All of Our Affairs

Committed at Work

Challenge:

One of the most important contributions one can make to a romantic relationship is to be present in body, mind and spirit. This can be difficult to do when one or both of the partners are not practicing the principles of recovery in all of their affairs. Many would like to hold to the old injunction that work should be kept at work and "home business" excluded from work. It is a rational enough philosophy; only, it never really works that way. If you are troubled at work you will bring those feelings and thoughts home with you to your relationship. If you deal with your difficulties at work by being manipulative and assassinating colleague's characters, you will bring those practices home with you. Many agree that it is far easier to be committed at our 12 Step meeting than it is at work. Our work environments can hold many challenges to our pursuit of the knowledge of our God's will for us. We sometimes indulge in character assassination as a "survival tactic" with the justification that it is a natural part of office politics.

Reflection:

It is sometimes difficult to see, but the roles we play at work will eventually influence our personal relationships outside of work. Most of us readily accept the idea of "one God." That God may come to us in a variety of different forms, but we are never confused about whether or not it is him. We can tell him by his works. The same is true for us. There can only be one version of us. We cannot behave differently at a meeting than we behave at work.

Prayer:

God, help me to remain one with you in all of my affairs.

In All of Our Affairs

Committed at Play

Challenge:

When two people form a relationship, they bring many different experiences and diverging interests with them. Many partners will have their lives enriched by the interests that their mate brings to the union. Unfortunately, some relationships will be weakened by the varied interests of the two partners when recreational interests are pursued in a solitary or exclusionary fashion.

Reflection:

Separate interest can be complementary to the relationship, but separate relationships are not. Look for opportunities to recreate together. When shared recreational times are not possible or desirable, look for ways of sharing your love for the activity. We do not have to do everything together, but everything we do can be brought back to the relationship.

Prayer:

God, be with us in all that we do. Show me how to share my life fully with my partner.

In All of Our Affairs

Committed at Service

Challenge:

A romantic relationship can be a beacon that guides others to God's love or a lighthouse to warn others away from danger. When your relationship is one of conflict, disharmony and hostility, others will stay clear. The negativity and depressive dynamics of a conflicted relationship will not be attractive to other couples seeking a better life together.

Reflection:

Your romantic partnership can be a wondrous example of God-centered service. Troubled couples could find rest in the harbor created by God's love moving through the two of you. If you are committed to each other, others will derive strength from you. Allow the God of your understanding to forge a deeper commitment in your union through your united service to others. Be one in the spirit and let your spiritual union point others to the God of their understanding.

Prayer:

God, bring us opportunities to be of service to others through the strength of our common bond.

In All of Our Affairs

One Me

Challenge:

When our behavior changes from one environment to the next, we will become deeply confused. When the expression of our values and beliefs change with the circumstances we find ourselves in, we will become lost. When we portray different versions of ourselves, we will lose our identity, hope and sense of purpose.

Reflection:

Who we are and what we believe is most closely reflected in how we behave. How we behave must look the same in every aspect of our lives. We cannot be a couple only during times of mutual need or sexual intimacy. We must be a couple when we are shopping, paying the bills, recreating, serving others, and praying. If we are different in different circumstances, we are not a couple.

Prayer:

God, help me to be true to you, to my partner, and true to myself.

In All of Our Affairs

Weekend Workshop

There can be only one version of our romantic relationship. We cannot treat each other with the utmost dignity and respect when we are alone and with disregard and indifference when we are in the company of our friends. We cannot treat each other with warmth and tenderness when we are sexually engaged and ignore each other's needs for help with chores. If there is going to be only one version of "us" we should have that version be the version that we would display if our God came to dinner. We hope you are working toward a romance that is the same no matter where you go or whom you are with.

John & Elaine

My Gifts to the Partnership

Examine yourself closely to identify the ways that you change your behavior in the relationship and in ways that might diminish the perceived value of your partner.

Share your discoveries with a member of your support group.

Explore one of the changes you discovered in the above task with your partner. Practice only self-disclosure and do not offer or solicit input.

Plans, Not Expectations

Our Unclear Past

Challenge:

None of us can accurately predict or control the future. We can try to manipulate the variables in life to have a certain desired outcome come our way but, more times than not, the ending is not what we desired. Many of us will direct our behavior and the lives of those close to us in an effort to avoid repeating the past. We want to be rid of the life we had and not look back. We are cautioned to learn from our past or be doomed by it. So why do we run from it?

Reflection:

When we run from the past, it will teach us nothing. When we attempt to manipulate the future, the harvest will be unfulfilling. We need to examine our past loves to better understand how to love fully today. We must trust our future to God's care if we want to avoid making the same mistakes. An understanding of our past will generate the calm you need today to allow the gifts of the future to be revealed.

Prayer:

God, help me to be honest about where I have been so the future will hold promise and not fear.

Plans, Not Expectations

Uncharted Future

Challenge:

The fact that our future is uncharted will be a reality that generates either fear or excitement. Many in our fellowships speak of a dreaded fear of the "unknown" which, for some, can be paralyzing. Although we understand the intended meaning of this fear, it has little real meaning. How can we really be afraid of the "unknown?" The "unknown" exists on a busy street as the cars wiz past and a small child emerges between two parked cars unaware of the danger. The unknown can be hazardous for the child, but they are not afraid. The child has no life experience to suggest that what they can't see might hurt them. If we are afraid of what we can't see, it is because we have known disappointment.

Reflection:

The uncharted seas ahead of us can hold great adventure and opportunity for enormous growth and success. There will be disappointment – that is a given. What we do not know is how we will reinvest the treasure that lays just below the crest of fear.

Prayer:

God, help me to look to the future with awe and wonder.

Plans, Not Expectations

Expressing Our Needs & Wants

Challenge:

As a couple, our shared needs and wants can provide us with inspiration during times of strain and faith during times of fear. When we expect that our partner should anticipate our wants and prepare for our needs, we are likely to precipitate rejection and stimulate resentment.

Reflection:

Faulty advertising has led us to believe that true love ensures the anticipation of desires and the fulfillment of needs. When we take the risk to express our wants to our partner, we are generating romance. When we rely on our partner to assist in the fulfillment of our expressed needs, we are cultivating intimacy.

Prayer:

God, help me to help my partner know me as you do.

Plans, Not Expectations

Team Planning

Challenge:

Surprise parties are great fun and harmless acts of deception, which generally leave the honored person feeling quite special. Most other forms of deception will leave one or both of the romantic partners feeling mistrustful and unloved.

Reflection:

A healthy romantic partnership will require that each partner maintain 100% responsibility for the tasks and 50% of the voting stock. We can neither assign nor assume duties; they must be planned for. We cannot delegate or relegate responsibility. We must assume responsibility, not authority. If neither one of us holds 51% of the stock, then the authority will rest with the God of our understanding. If each member of the relationship assumed 100% of the responsibility for the relationship then neither would be able to blame the other for what did or did not get accomplished. In a full partnership, there are no preconceived assumptions about roles, tasks, or obligations. There are only preferences and sacrifices. In a full partnership, one partner cannot outvote or bully the other partner. If each partner holds 50% of the stock then they will have to find a compromise.

Prayer:

God, help me to understand the meaning of a full partnership.

Plans, Not Expectations

Progress, Not Perfection

Challenge:

This union we are forging will become stronger with time. We will continue to make progress if it is perfection that we seek. When we lower our sights, we slow our progress. Keeping the bar high will not frustrate you as much as you might think. When we place the bar slightly beyond our reach, we will grow stronger, our efforts will grow stronger, and our efforts will be more handsomely rewarded.

Reflection:

We have made great strides in the development of honesty, openness and willingness. We stand ready to meet the challenges as they arise because we are committed to a more perfect union. We have made much progress and greater riches await us. We will not rest too long—progress is waiting to be made.

Prayer:

God, help me to keep my eyes on the prize.

Plans, Not Expectations

Weekend Workshop

Few phrases chill the spine of a romance in the way that, "If you loved me ..." does. If you are on the receiving end of that line you know that you are being judged and that something is being expected of you. If you are the sender it can be assumed that you are hurt and that your expectations have been spoiled. We discovered, after much hardship, that the truer measure of love was our willingness to tell each other what we desired rather than test that person's love by their ability to read our minds. We pray that you make plans with enthusiasm and childhood wonder and restrict your expectations of your partner to their willingness to work on his/her relationship with his/her Higher Power.

John & Elaine

My Gifts to the Partnership

Describe, in writing, your historical struggle with expectations. Focus specifically on the romantic expectations that you have been disappointed by.

Plan an exotic escape with your partner as if you had the money and time to support it. Where would you go and what would you do? What did you learn about yourself in the planning?

Natural and Logical Consequences for Couples

Avoiding Punishment

Challenge:

None of us deserve to be hurt and none of us have the right to get even. Hammurabi introduced us to a revenge based formula to redress wrongs. His code includes the concept of taking an "eye for an eye" and a "tooth for a tooth." When our partner has committed a wrong that we have felt injured by, we have the option of planning for our response or reacting to the injury. Proponents of punishment would advise that we act swiftly and in a decisive manner that ensures that the wrong will not be repeated. Before you act, consider the benefit of punishment, but punish quickly because the benefit quickly fades with the act of retribution.

Reflection:

There is no indication that the death penalty deters would-be murderers. What we do know about punishment is that it teaches the perpetrator that if they are willing to do the time they can continue to do the crime. When the accused is a loved one, our punishment seldom matches the "crime" as we are reacting from our emotions and not our intellect. If you avoid punishment, you will decrease the supply of available hurt.

Prayer:

God, help me to not judge my partner.

Natural and Logical Consequences for Couples

Pain Creates a Long, but Unreliable, Memory

Challenge:

The principles of natural and logical consequences provide meaningful alternatives to the spiritually-starved acts of retaliation so many of us have become accustomed to. A natural consequence occurs naturally in the environment like the bad breath that prevents the good night kiss because we have neglected our dental hygiene. Logical consequences, like the act of withdrawing support from a loved one who is hurtful, are derived from the balance between our emotions and our intellect. Punishment evolves from pain in an effort to "get even." The problem with this approach is that we are generally going to "get even" for all the harms ever caused by all the perpetrators in our life – not just the accused.

Reflection:

Before you "get even," make sure you know which wrong you are attempting to right. Does your accused deserve what you have planned for him/her or is he/she paying for the injuries caused by others?

Prayer:

God, help me to see methods for stopping the cycle of revenge.

Natural and Logical Consequences for Couples

The Laws of Nature

Challenge:

The prospect of permitting a loved one to learn from his/her mistakes can raise great fear. When we punish with the rationalization that "this is for his/her own good," we are attempting to teach the person a "lesson" that they would learn naturally if we got out of the way. It could be argued that the lesson that we are trying to teach is really designed to benefit us and not the accused, but we will address that issue in another meditation. When we resort to punishment, we teach the accused to avoid punishment and not the unwanted behavior.

Reflection:

The undesirable behaviors we seek to punish have a function and a purpose for the person creating the harm. If we punish the behavior, there will be no incentive for the accused to examine the defects of character that are at the root of the behavior. If you want to help them, offer to help. Punishment is not help no matter how you dress it up.

Prayer:

God, help me to allow the natural and logical consequences of my unbridled defects of character show me what needs to change.

Natural and Logical Consequences for Couples

Avoiding Rewards

Challenge:

We sometimes get lulled into believing that the sacrifices we make for a loved one should be acknowledged. We tend to look for indications that our efforts to serve have been noticed and appreciated. We feel we need to know that our partner has had the realization that we have done something for him/her. Why is it that we place so much emphasis on rewards and praise? If you spend time keeping score of your partner's reaction to your behavior, you will have a difficult time keeping the records accurate. You may be very good at knowing what is owed you, but you will be easily confused about who it is that owes you. If you find yourself saying, "he/she doesn't appreciate me" then it is likely that you do not feel appreciated in other areas of your life. We tend to hold our romantic partners responsible for filling the emotional and spiritual holes in us. This "accounting" will be dangerous because your feelings might not know who has failed to acknowledge you and you can easily fall into the trap of placing blame on your partner for what someone else has failed to do for you.

Reflection:

Why have we done the deed? Why have we been of service? If we have done the deed for our partner, we are apt to look for a reward for our efforts and our sacrifices. If we have done the deed to serve some need in ourselves, we will never get sufficient acknowledgement from our partner. If we have done the deed as an act of service to the God of our understanding, we will be rewarded immediately and we will not have the need for sophisticated recordkeeping practices to be sure that we are getting what we have coming to us. Your God always pays.

Prayer:

God, help me to keep my eye on the needs you have of me regardless of who the acts of service are directed towards. I trust that you know my heart when I am serving you and I do not need to keep score.

Natural and Logical Consequences for Couples

Glory to God

Challenge:

The recognition we seek from our fellows and our partner can be a natural human response to our desire to be affirmed in what we believe or how we are acting. When we look to our loved ones to help us better understand our motives and expectations, the behavior can be quite healthy. When we look to our partner for acknowledgment of our acceptability when the affirmation needs to come from a true Higher Power, we will often be disappointed. We may get the recognition that we asked for or the affirmation that we were sure we needed from our partner, but in the end we are left feeling unfulfilled. This lack of acknowledgement tends to leave many of us with the misunderstanding that our partner has not met our needs; we feel rejected, and pull away.

Reflection:

Many times the lack of acknowledgement we have been left with is not a product of our partner's having "done it wrong" or not done it at all. The disappointment we are left with can be a symptom of having gone to the wrong source of potential approval and recognition. It is a common trap. Our Higher Power's rewards can be difficult to measure as they are not tangible and usually are not felt with the flesh. At the same time, those rewards will come to all of us if we are willing to give him the glory for the things we have done. This can be a difficult concept to accept. We will be fulfilled when our God gets the praise that we are seeking for ourselves. These rewards will become more real as we acknowledge them through further service.

Prayer:

God, help me to give you the glory.

Natural and Logical Consequences for Couples

Weekend Workshop

Our decision to allow the natural and logical consequences of life to be the parenting tutor helped us to avoid the praise/punishment paradigm that we had been trapped in as new parents. We wanted desperately to raise our children differently than we had been raised but we did not know what we were doing. When we stopped asking ourselves what a "parent should do" the answers came to us. We began to apply the principles to the rest of our relationships and resigned from the burden of "judge, jury, and executioner." We pray that you surrender those role expectations or duties if you are still burdened by them.

John & Elaine

My Gifts to the Partnership

What lesson, that you believe your partner really needs to learn, are you willing to give up trying to teach him/her?

What lesson, that your partner has been trying to teach you, are you now willing to learn? Share the lesson that you are now willing to learn with your partner.

How Much Is Enough

When Too Much Is Not Enough

Challenge:

We have all known the pain of unmet emotional needs in a romantic relationship. When we are dissatisfied in a relationship, we tend to look at the other person for an explanation for the deprivation that we are experiencing. During the high times when we are feeling nearly content, we find ourselves on the lookout for the next serving of love, attention, or affection. We are filled up, but our fear tells us that we need just a little bit more. During low times, our hunger for attention is ravenous and we are certain that we will starve if we do not have the opportunity to gorge ourselves on the attention of our partner. In either case, the demands we make will get louder and more desperate; even when our partner responds, we might feel cheated because we, in our perception, have been forced to wait too long.

Reflection:

How much is enough? When will we ever be filled and have security? Seldom is the hunger for emotional attention imagined. If you feel it is real, it is real. Do not scold yourself for having "unrealistic expectations." The need for attention is real but the hunger may not be coming from perceived lack of volume. The problem is not with the size of the portions we are offered by those who love us. In reality, the problem may be that we are attempting to derive satisfaction from a relationship with our partner that is needed in some other relationships. In many cases, it is not human attention that we yearn for, but a bonding with a spiritual power. When the hunger is for greater spiritual nourishment, humans will disappoint us.

Prayer:

God, help me to eat my fill at your table before I measure what others are contributing to my life.

How Much Is Enough

When Too Little Is Painful

Challenge:

Lack of love, attention, and affection can be painful and contribute to the deterioration and break up of a romantic relationship. Some relationships end in a traumatic event; others seem to just wither away. When a relationship ends in infidelity, it is common to hear from the "injured party" that he/she never saw it coming. In the shock and rage that follows the discovery of the affair, all mental records of past hurts are replaced by the gaping chest wound created by betrayal. Was there no warning? Was there no feeling of separation or disconnectedness? The "unfaithful" partner often claims that he/she, too, did not see "it" coming. Sometimes they claim to be nearly as surprised as the "injured party" by what has happened. How could the relationship have deteriorated to the point of infidelity and dissolution with neither partner knowing it?

Reflection:

It is not true that the partners in a romantic relationship are the last to know that the relationship is in trouble. We know when our partner is pulling away. We know when we are feeling deprived of attention or affection. We know when we are flirting with others or being the object of someone else's flirtation. Flirtation is the act of pretending that the parties involved are in a relationship. It is not harmless. It is romantic poison. When the "emotional phone" is ringing, you need to answer it. If the relationship is generating pain, you need to address it. When we wait too long, we do not notice the little bits of pain. We eventually will see and feel the pain when the relationship ends, but it should not be a surprise.

Prayer:

God, help me to respond to what I see and feel, even when I do not have proof.

How Much Is Enough

Measuring My Worth

Challenge:

Both partners in a relationship have strengths that they contribute to the relationship, as well as weaknesses that pose challenges to the security of the union. If we compare our weaknesses to the strengths of our partner, we will undervalue our worth as a person and the value of our contribution to the romance. Conversely, if we compare our strengths to our partner's weaknesses, we will overvalue our contribution to the relationship and fail to see our partner's value as a partner and mate. The tendency to look for ways to measure our worth by the reception we receive from a romantic partner is common. We say to ourselves that we "must not be worthy" or he/she would not be so unavailable. Our practice of measuring our worth by evaluating other people's behavior toward us can be very unhealthy.

Reflection:

Our needs for emotional and spiritual security can place an unbearable burden on a romance, especially if it is in the fragile state of rebuilding, as is often the case in the beginning of recovery. Our personal worth can be bolstered if we are treating others, as God would have us treat them. If we are practicing our Higher Power's will for us in our relationship with others, we will recognize our value and appreciate our worth. Likewise, when we guide others to treat us with love and kindness, our sense of personal worth will grow.

Prayer:

God, help me to examine the nature of my relationships with others for a more accurate measurement of my worth.

How Much Is Enough

Identify, Do Not Compare

Challenge:

The tendency to measure our individual worth by comparing what we have with what others have acquired or accumulated is fairly common. The practice of comparing our "stuff" to other's "stuff" is a particularly dangerous practice when it comes to our romantic relationship. When our romance is great, all is wonderful and our partner is perfect. When our relationship becomes hard work or is challenged by the demands of health problems, economic insecurity or other uncontrollable stumbling blocks, it is easy to begin comparing our mate to the possibilities we see around us. With each act of romantic comparison that we indulge in, the gap between our mate and ourselves widens. When we begin to imagine (fantasize) what it would be like to change partners, we can develop the harmful illusion that relationships can simply be replaced when they become difficult. If you are comparing your relationship to others you have had or those you desire, you will lose the romantic spirit that provides motivation when things are difficult.

Reflection:

Comparison is unhealthy as we generally are guilty of comparing our insides with other people's outsides. We imagine that we will acquire the happiness that we see in others by simply obtaining the elements that we see in their picture. If we had their romantic partner, their house, their car, their life, then ours would be better. The reality is that we do not know what their life is like by viewing the outside picture. Get to know the people whose life you desire and perhaps you will be able to identify with them more than you expect.

Prayer:

God, help me to identify, rather than compare. I do not know what it is like to be anyone but me.

How Much Is Enough

Spiritual Yardstick

Challenge:

When the answer to the question, "How much is enough?" is eluding you, it is time for concern. The tendency for people to define themselves by how much they earn, what they weigh, or who wants to be their friend is problematic for everyone, but dangerous for those in recovery. The tendency for recovering individuals to be tempted into relapse because they feel like they do not measure up is not uncommon. When the feeling of emptiness intensifies it is likely that we will think about old ways of filling the hole. We have lived in the hell that other people fear themselves sinking into when they do not measure up. For us, thinking about returning to a mood-altering behavior for the purpose of "being more" is suicidal. We cannot measure ourselves or our progress by the outward pictures that others present. We will not measure up. We must measure ourselves against a more predictable, realistic reference point.

Reflection:

The most reliable reference point is your God's love. God's love for us is an absolute that we can always count on being there, especially when we feel unlovable. One presentation of this love for us is the way in which he makes his will for us known as a guidepost for sober living. When you are suspect that you are not enough, go into meditation to discern what God's will for you is and you will immediately see how you measure up. Trust your heart, not your eyes.

Prayer:

God, help me to look to you when I want to know what I am worth.

How Much Is Enough

For as long as either one of us could remember, we have struggled with the meaning of enough. It seems to be such a relative term. If we are with people who have a lot, then ours is not enough. If we are with people who have a little, then ours is too much. At the core of the problem has been the ever-elusive goal of balance. The maintenance of balance between the needs of the body, mind, and spirit remain a significant challenge for each of us. We are not sure that balance is ever sustainable. We suspect that the true measure of balance lies in the pursuit of it. We pray that you never tire of working for balance.

John & Elaine

My Gifts to the Partnership

Make a list of the stuff that you were once sure that you would need to be happy and compare it to stuff that brings you happiness today.

Identify something that you cannot ever seem to get enough of and give it up for a month in order to see what it means to you.

Share with your partner the ways that he/she has surpassed your expectation of love.

Vocations & Avocations

I Am More than What I Do for a Living

Challenge:

Many times, couples find that their bond is threatened by the occupational roles they have assumed. Occupational demands, regardless of their origin, can become consuming. It is easy to assume the role of the homemaker or corporate executive in our romantic relationships. The roles may involve similar tasks and both contribute equally to the overall welfare of the family, but they will promote instability in a romance. There is no place for executive decisions in a romance. Exclusive caretaking by one partner results in an imbalance.

Reflection:

A healthy romance does not need anyone "in charge." Executive decisions require authority and that does not exist in a true romantic partnership. Caretaking is always uneven and will create helplessness. Care giving will promote interdependence that is vital to the health of a relationship.

Prayer:

God, help me to understand that I am far more than what I do for a living.

Vocations & Avocations

Balance Is Not a Dirty Word

Challenge:

The maintenance of balance in our recoveries between duty, service, and play is an ongoing struggle for most of us. Many times, the needs of a romantic relationship end up at the bottom of our priority list. Occupational tasks demand our attention. Childrearing responsibilities can sometimes drain our spirits. Holidays generate obligations, which can appear to occur in a continuous stream with no breaks. Family emergencies seem to occur at all the wrong times and calls to 12 Step service have been known to interrupt many a cuddle time.

Reflection:

If we leave the needs of our romance for last, there will be no romance. A romance is like a living organism. When it is nurtured, it will thrive and generate increased sources of energy to draw upon when responding to the other calls we receive.

Prayer:

God, help me to include my romance as an altar of service to you.

Vocations & Avocations

House Calls: Serving at Home

Challenge:

The spiritual awakening which we are experiencing is opening our eyes to the needs of others. For many of us, the idea of putting others before ourselves is an alien concept. The journey of recovery has taught us that failure to serve others can be hazardous to our recovery. We have learned to look for opportunities to be of service.

Reflection:

If we provide service to others and dismiss the needs of those intimately involved in our lives, our safety and security will be threatened. Romantic relationships become sanctuaries when they are places of mutual support and intimate positive regard. When romantic relationships are ignored, the safety they offer fades and the feeling of sanctuary is replaced with one of exile. We can be together and alone or together and united – the choice is ours.

Prayer:

God, help me to serve at home so that home remains a safe place.

Vocations & Avocations

The Most Important Job

Challenge:

We are frequently reminded that romance, however passionate, can be hard work. The work of romance is not merely in the problem-solving challenges, or the struggle associated with our defects of character. For romance to grow, we must take risks associated with spontaneity. We must expose the relationship to the scrutiny of our most trusted fellows. We must be willing to place our romance ahead of all human relationships. It must be second only to self-care and service to our Higher Power. There are many other tasks that pale in comparison to the need to have our romantic relationship be an extension of our Higher Power's love for us.

Reflection:

The most important job that each of us has is to love others as our God continues to love us. To what degree can others see your God's love present in your romance?

Prayer:

God, help me to make my romance a testimony of your love for me.

Vocations & Avocations

Serving God

Challenge:

Our vocational and avocational desires create a path with many intersections. The decisions we make at those intersections will result in experiences that are exhilarating and those that are deeply troubling. The joy that we discover can contribute to the strengthening of our romantic union or jealousy. The burdens we face can be diminished by sharing them with our partner or exacerbated by assuming that we must face them alone.

Reflection:

If we decide to serve the God of our understanding in both our vocations and our avocations, we must remember that the key to service as a couple is that our efforts be a reflection of our love for each other. Involve your romantic relationship in the intimate details of your service to your Higher Power and your fellows, and your romance will be a reflecting pond for your God's love.

Prayer:

God, help me to see how I can promote your image to others.

Vocations & Avocations

Weekend Workshop

Each one of us is more than what people can see. We once found ourselves being defined as people by the tasks that we performed both inside and outside of our home. We were, at the time, more like "human doings" than we were "human beings." It was a sad but necessary discovery that opened the door to opportunities to pursue our dreams. Are you doing or being?

John & Elaine

My Gifts to the Partnership

Make a list with two columns. In one column place the tasks that you do that explain who you are as a person. In the other column place the tasks that you do that confuse the picture of who you are as a person.

Share both of your lists with your partner and tell your partner about the tasks that he/she performs that impresses you.

Love Can Not Be Tested

Love Can Not Be Tested

Challenge:

When we were teenagers, we all experimented with the deceptive tactics that we assumed would extract the truth from those we cared for. We were certain that the only way to uncover the feelings of a prospective romantic partner was to ask others or conduct field tests. We would ask a friend to find out whether or not objects of our romantic interest were attracted to us. When there were no "reliable" sources of information, we would arrange tests that would attempt to evoke a jealous reaction, which would assure us of the person's attraction to us. The relationships we acquired through these deceptive means seldom lasted, but that was all right because we were young.

Reflection:

Many of us have learned little from our youth. We continue to play games and test our partners' love. The tests may be more sophisticated, but the outcomes are the same. The life expectancy of the relationship is shortened. Romantic tests are conducted when we expect to find flaws in our partner's commitment. When we become insecure, we test again and again. We will eventually find flaws in any relationship. If flaws are what will send us running, we might as well remain alone.

Prayer:

God, help me to ask directly for the answers that I seek.

Love Can Not Be Tested

How Do I Know that God Loves Me

Challenge:

Many of us were instructed as children not to question our God's love for us. We were told that we were alive because he loved us. For some of us, the quality of our childhood lives left us not only questioning that love, but also wondering if he really existed. How could there be a God who would allow all this pain? As we grew up, we developed a longing for a romantic partner to share our lives with, but found only heartache and rejection. "Where was this God of love?" we wondered.

Reflection:

Our God is not a puppeteer who moves us in and out of pain and joy according to some grand scheme or for his personal amusement. We have been given the ability to receive and block love through the expression of our free will. We must decide which choice to make. The walls we designed to keep out the pain also keep out life.

Prayer:

God, help me to acknowledge your love for me through the expression of my love to others.

Love Can Not Be Tested

What Is It that You Are Really Testing

Challenge:

When we devise a test to determine if we are truly loved by our partner, we are placing the relationship at great risk. The "If he/she really loved me…" scenarios we run through our minds will dim the light surrounding our partner and cause us to view him/her with suspicion. When we employ manipulative behaviors to discover our partner's true feelings for us, we generally cause the walls of distrust and defensiveness to get thicker.

Reflection:

If you must test your partner's love and commitment, then it is likely that you do not know what "proof" you are looking for and you will not know how to evaluate your findings. Have you tested your partner's love or have you tested how well your partner takes the test? It may be that your test results prove your partner does not love you; however it might be that he/she does not know how to love you the way you want to be loved. As an alternative to testing, consider communicating directly with your partner about the ways that you like to be loved and the ways that you like to demonstrate your love.

Prayer:

God, help me to end the game-playing; for there can be no winners, only losers.

Love Can Not Be Tested

Chronic Insecurity

Challenge:

Our desire to test our partner's love for us may be founded in an insecurity that he/she cannot satisfy. When we are chronically unsure of where we stand in the life of another, the problem most likely is within us. The emotional threat we hope to calm with a test of our partner may be emanating from conflict and stress in other areas of our lives. When our spiritual reserves are depleted or we have failed to practice the principles of recovery in all of our affairs, emptiness will grow which demands attention. We often assume that attention must come from our romantic partner.

Reflection:

No one person or relationship can fill all of our holes. When we pursue a strategy of getting our "needs" met through our romance, we will bring a burden so heavy on that relationship that it may not withstand the test.

Prayer:

God, help me to examine my recovery when it seems like my partner is failing me.

Love Can Not Be Tested

Letting God Be the Judge

Challenge:

Every day young couples stand before a clergy person or a justice of the peace and commit themselves to their partners in marriage. Their vows are made official and married life begins. Fifty-one percent of these couples will divorce within four years. So, what is the problem? Fingers are pointed in every direction. Some blame goes to financial burdens that are said to erode the union and some is assigned to the strain of childrearing that weakens the couple's commitment to each other. Still others blame "society." Where does the fault lie?

Reflection:

Why do we insist on looking outside of the relationship for an explanation of what eroded the core commitment each partner had vowed to each other? We can argue that it is too easy to get divorced, or we can contend that it is too easy to get married. The couple may have made commitments before a representative of their God and then failed to ask their God directly if their union was in keeping with his will for them.

Prayer:

God, help me to come to you to judge my behavior in the relationship. In that way I will know if our union is a service to you.

Love Can Not Be Tested

We entered our relationship with very little trust in romance or commitment and a fear of relying on anyone for support or security. In pursuit of reassurance, we required that our partner could be trusted, and we conjured up many tests. The tests were applied without much regard for our partner because he/she was not told that an evaluation was being conducted. We hurt each other a great deal in order to assuage the fear each of us had of being hurt by the other. Love is a decision that two people share in. If one person does not love the other, there is nothing that can be done to alter that reality and the truth will be revealed in time. Ask the questions you want answers to and accept the response you receive without judgment. No test is needed.

John & Elaine

My Gifts to the Partnership

Make a list that describes every test you ever initiated to evaluate someone's trustworthiness. What were the outcomes and what were the costs? Were they worth it?

Share with your partner the ways that you demonstrate your commitment to him/her. Your partner is not to agree or disagree with your presentation, only to receive it as an expression of your openness.

Healing Our Troubled Past

We Will Not Regret the Past

Challenge:

Our relationship, whether it is new or old, will be continually challenged by the experiences of our past. The joys and sorrows we have known are sure to surface as our current relationship becomes more intimate. We can shut the door to our past, but it will always find a way into the present. When we experience disappointment with our partner, our feeling memories remind us that we have known this pain before. When we are tenderly held by our partner, we will be filled with hope one minute and reminded of desperate moments in our past the next.

Reflection:

If we keep the door open to our past, we will have the opportunity to learn from it and change the course of the present. The wounds of our past will begin to heal in the warmth and tenderness of our current relationship.

Prayer:

God, help me to remain a student of all that I have experienced as well as that which I have yet to discover.

Healing Our Troubled Past

Know Our Common Wounds

Challenge:

Many of us have spent time lamenting the romantic choices we have made. We vow to do it differently every time we begin a new relationship. Somehow, every relationship seems to end up the same. We think we are diabolically attracted to people who are incapable of meeting our needs. It is more likely however, that we are attracted to people who have similar needs. They are no better equipped to get them met than we are.

Reflection:

If we are attracted to mates with similar needs, then it is probably because they have endured similar injuries. When we really get to understand each other's wounds, we will discover ways to share in the healing.

Prayer:

God, help me to have the courage to expose all of me to my partner so that I may become a part of the solution.

Healing Our Troubled Past

Solution or Problem: You Decide

Challenge:

Our romantic future will be largely dependent on our approach to life's challenges. If we respond to the stresses of everyday life with dread, we will have many problems. If we retreat from the darker side of our partner's character rather than embrace it as a student, we might become a prisoner of the places we hide inside. If we avoid the romantic challenges that arise when building an intimate relationship, we will miss the opportunities to correct the behaviors that created crisis in our past.

Reflection:

We are going to be a part of the solution or we will become part of the problem. This time-honored slogan for living is one we generally remember after a romantic crisis has lessened. If we adopt the position of building a solution during a crisis, we will have far fewer amends to make.

Prayer:

God, help me to bring clarity to times of confusion before I help those times become crises.

Healing Our Troubled Past

Cleansing the Wounds Might Be Painful

Challenge:

All of us can remember the somewhat less-than-comforting introduction to a distasteful medicine. "This may be a little hard to swallow, but it will be good for you." None of us ever really believed that the "cure" was going to be good for us. We were too inexperienced to make the connection between the relief of a symptom and the relief that followed the bad-tasting remedy. We took the medicine because we had to, not because the promise of health was reassuring. It would seem, in retrospect, that the promise of relief was designed to relieve the stress our caregiver was experiencing.

Reflection:

Our adult recovery experiences have shown us many times what we could not see as kids: wounds and symptoms had to be cleansed and treated for the pain to subside. What we accept about our physical recovery from injury, we must also apply to the emotional wounds we endure. The cleansing may be painful, but it is necessary for the relief we seek.

Prayer:

God, help me to approach every cleansing with the faith I was deprived of in my youth. All wounds can be healed, but not without pain.

Healing Our Troubled Past

Avoiding New Injuries

Challenge:

The past can be a wise teacher, but not if we continue to repeat it. We will learn nothing from repeating the same behaviors over and over again. Just as we will learn nothing from that insight, we continue to repeat the past while expecting the results to be different. Pain does not produce change; it only provides us with insight into an area that needs to be addressed. Insight does not result in change. The only way to change is to change.

Reflection:

The way to initiate lasting change in our personality and in our love relationships is to undertake a "different way" when the "same old way" looks seductively inviting. The work we must take on lies in the forgotten 6th and 7th Steps of our program! When we approach these steps with the conviction we had in the 1st step, we will make the changes that make it difficult for us to continue generating the same old injuries.

Prayer:

God, help me to replace the regrets of doing the same old thing with the hope we will find in taking the 6th and 7th Step with you.

Healing Our Troubled Past

Weekend Workshop

We have joked about our shared perception that God brought us together in order to prevent us from doing any more romantic harm to other prospective partners. All kidding aside, it was hurtful to examine the ways we had injured others in romance and we do not take the self-exploration lightly. Over the years, we have taken the inventories that were needed and made the amends that we were permitted to make. In many ways, the Step work we completed around the romances of our respective lives was crucial to our romantic bond. It was, however, the risks that we took to expose ourselves to each other that began the process of healing our troubled past. We pray that you depend on each other to be the tools for healing that your Higher Power intended.

John & Elaine

My Gifts to the Partnership

Describe the contribution that your partner has made to your recovery that promoted the greatest healing for you and share it with a member of your support group.

Share the journal entry you created in the above task with your partner.

Common Denominator

Partners Are Not Problems

Challenge:

Many of our romantic relationships look painfully similar. We often attribute the mirror-like similarities to some facet of our personality that causes us to choose emotionally unavailable partners. If all of our relationships seem to end the same way regardless of how they begin, we are right to assume that there is a common problem. We complain that all of them are "too controlling" or "too dependent," or "too independent." A close examination of the problem is necessary if we ever expect to find romantic happiness. And so it begins...

Reflection:

The problem cannot be explained by the similarities in the partners we choose. We must turn our attention to the common denominator – us. How is our behavior the same from one romance to the next? If we want to change the outcome, we must change the input.

Prayer:

God, help me to see what I need to change in order to enjoy a fulfilling romance.

Common Denominator

The Person I Was...

Challenge:

The person I was will fall again. We can regret our past misbehavior, but it will not change the relationship that we are in and it will not prevent us from committing the same mistakes. If the person I was will fall again, perhaps a focused inventory of our past and present romantic relationships will reveal the patterns of our maladaptive behavior that are cheating us out of romantic happiness.

Reflection:

The focused inventory should explore both the hurts that we have endured, as well as the wrongs we have perpetrated. When we have done a thorough housecleaning and shared our discoveries with our God and another human being, we will acquire a framework for addressing the defects in our character that undermine our romantic success.

Prayer:

God, help me to see what I need to change and share the truth with others as it is revealed to me.

Common Denominator

Came to Believe...

Challenge:

If a power greater than ourselves can restore us to sanity, that same power can reveal the root of our romantic insanity if only we ask. Many of us have been amazed at the degree of romantic instability that can be present when much of the rest of our life looks pretty normal. This disparity is common because we tend to work harder at becoming the best parent, employee and 12 Step group member than we do at being the best lover we can be. Sometimes we avoid the work involved in growing as a lover because we do not know what to do. Other times we avoid working on being a better lover because we do not believe that we can change what is broken in us.

Reflection:

The belief that we can not change what is broken is a good place to stop and examine how much stock we have misplaced over the years in attempting to improve our power. It was there in the 3rd Step all along. All we needed was willingness.

Prayer:

God, help me to look to you for the power to change. I now have the willingness.

Common Denominator

The Wisdom to Know the Difference

Challenge:

We have enjoyed the guidance available in the Serenity Prayer for many years. It has provided us with a method of deciding on a course of action when we found ourselves flustered and confused. We needed only to choose to change the things that we could change and God would provide us with the power, if only we asked. The same prayer can be used to guide us through the labyrinth of issues that arise during the development of an intimate romantic relationship. So, why is it so infrequently used during times of romantic difficulty?

Reflection:

There is no need for the Serenity Prayer in our love relationship because when something is wrong we know who is wrong – our partner. If there is always something to change about our partner, then it stands to reason that they are the only one that needs to change. If we adhere to this practice, we are not likely to obtain the serenity that has been promised.

Prayer:

God, help me to look at only what needs to change about me.

Common Denominator

Lowest Common Denominator

Challenge:

We have explored the importance of self-examination in all aspects of our romantic life. Without a willingness to focus on the changes we must make, our romantic relationships will all end the same. Once we have learned to keep the focus on ourselves, we can work at changing the denominator we contribute to our relationships.

Reflection:

The lowest common denominator that you can find is the God of your understanding that lies within you. If all that you do and say in your romantic relationship is a reflection of your Higher Power's will for you, you will accomplish a great deal. Our verbal and non-verbal communication with our romantic partner is a mirror–like reflection of our spiritual condition. Is your partner seeing the God in you, or your own self-will run riot?

Prayer:

God, help me to be an outward manifestation of your love in all that I do and say.

Common Denominator

Weekend Workshop

We spent many years looking for the right romantic partner and terrified that we would find them. It was clear that the problems that we were having with our respective mates were largely of our own doing, but that did not stop us from complaining that all the "good ones" had been taken. We had both resigned ourselves to a life of romantic "dryness" before we met each other. After we met, we were certain that we were supposed to grow old alone because both of us found the other incredibly imperfect. Despite all the flaws that we found in each other, we could not remain apart. One would have to suspect that our Higher Power got tired of hearing us complain. Either that or he got frustrated with the discontent that we were causing others so he put us together. We hope you will work hard to keep the focus on yourself. We can now see faults in ourselves we could only see in each other, in the beginning.

John & Elaine

My Gifts to the Partnership

Describe in writing the defects in your character that have been present in all of your romantic relationships.

Examine those personal defects closely and reflect on how you tried to blame the discomfort associated with them on past partners.

Share with your partner your personal defects of character that you used to blame on your past partners. It is suggested that you do not open the discussion of how those defects might be presenting themselves in your current relationship.

We Are More than Our Past

Common Injuries

Challenge:

It can be sad to reflect on our childhood. For many in recovery fellowships, the memories contain painful reminders of the time we spent alone. Often times, siblings are isolated from each other through the defensive dynamics of the illness in their families. It is common for these children to grow up with real difficulty expressing and receiving emotional intimacy. Many romantic relationships continue to play out the drama the respective partners lived in as children. It is little wonder that so many of our marriages end in divorce.

Reflection:

Our common injuries will draw us together initially as a deep, unspoken empathy is shared. This common bond together will not secure the success of our future. Eventually, the strategies that each partner developed to insulate them from hurt in the past will become destructive obstacles to lasting romantic success.

Prayer:

God, help me to exchange my old coping strategies with new methods for honest communication and intimate bonding.

We Are More than Our Past

Defects as Assets

Challenge:

The methods that we developed for coping with our developmental life experiences were vital to our survival as children. When we experienced painful rejection and told ourselves "that does not matter, I do not need them anyway!" we devised a mode for managing pain. When we hid the excitement of a rewarding experience, we wanted to avoid ridicule for "behaving like a braggart"; this false modesty would be an asset that kept us from being chastised.

Reflection:

Upon reflection, we can see that these assets, and many others, were the taproots of coping strategies that would later become harmful defects of character. If we can begin to expose these defects to our romantic partner, they will lose the power they seem to have over us.

Prayer:

God, help me to let go of past strategies for living that today serve only to create walls around me that keep me lonely.

We Are More than Our Past

Challenge:

It would be a fascinating experiment to travel back in time with our partners by our side to those life experiences from which we developed ways of "escaping." One would think that our partners, because of their common suffering, would prove to be an invaluable source of support and comfort. The probability however, even if time travel were possible, is that our partner would have been no more capable of rescuing us than we would them if the tables were turned.

Reflection:

There are many reasons for this hypothesis, but the most direct is that common suffering does little to promote understanding or empathy. As children, we experienced life in a uniqueness that left us being certain that we were the only ones going through it. We did not even confide in siblings or close friends. If we can begin sharing our identification with our partner, we will begin to see solutions together.

Prayer:

God, help me to focus my energy identification that will build a foundation for developing common solutions.

We Are More than Our Past

Problems Shared Cuts the Pain in Half

Challenge:

Who we are today is largely a measure of what we have experienced and how we have coped with it. While there is a great deal we can do about the way we cope with life, there is nothing we can do to change the life we have experienced. If we were victimized as children, it is likely that we will identify most with the role of the victim as adults. There are many examples of this "typecasting" that we accept to be our personality type. Our romantic future will be restricted by these boxes we climb into.

Reflection:

A personality may be the product of our life experiences, but we must remember that life is not over. We have many experiences in the present and the future that can serve to reshape our personality and the way that we view life. History cannot be changed, but it is being written every day. We have a choice in recovery to see ourselves as victims or survivors. If we want to be less defined by the pain of our past, we must share it with a loved one. The story of our survival is one that will create a healthy bond in a romance.

Prayer:

God, help me to cut my past down to the right size by sharing the pain.

We Are More than Our Past

Hope for the Future

Challenge:

As children, we would have had little access to hope. We knew hope as a verb when we hoped for a long-desired birthday present or vacation. We had little understanding of hope as a noun. The feeling of hope is much more than a desire. To have hope suggests that we have anticipated a negative outcome and experienced a desired one. The feeling of hope (a cousin of faith), comes when we are able, with the help of our Higher Power and our fellows, to overcome adversity. Some of us are still injured children who are afraid of having hope because we fear the feeling will evaporate when we are not looking.

Reflection:

A romantic relationship offers countless opportunities to replace isolated independence with mutual interdependence, which will awaken the excitement and spontaneity of our lost youth. Take a risk to experience hope.

Prayer:

God, help me to be available to have great things happen and show me where I can aid in their construction.

We Are More than Our Past

Weekend Workshop

We have come to accept that who we are is changing every day. Every day, life's challenges and our choices generate changes in us. We are not just the traumas we have survived or challenges we have faced. We are more than our resumes can describe and not always what others have thought of us. We have grown so much as a couple we are sometimes amazed. We have gotten so much more than we first bargained for. Over time, the bond that began as a "common suffering" has strengthened into a solid core of shared values that derives its mass from a commitment to serve our God. We hope the two of you continue on the journey you have begun.

John & Elaine

My Gifts to the Partnership

Write a paragraph or two that describes you without discussing your past, education, training, occupation, height, weight, annual income, religious affiliation, or age.

Go to a power greater than yourself in meditation and reflect on the values that make up the core of you.

Share your description of yourself with your partner.

God as We Understand Him

We Can Not Be God

Challenge:

Many of us enter recovery with a conflicted relationship with the God of our understanding. Others begin by denouncing the usefulness of pursuing a relationship with a Higher Power. Whatever your spiritual or religious beliefs, it is critical that you do not assume the role of a God in your romance. God-playing will involve acts of both manipulation and deception.

Reflection:

Your romance certainly needs a "Higher Power," but it cannot be either of the partners. The relationship's Higher Power can be the wisdom of the suggested spiritual principles you are living by. Some couples choose a seasoned recovering couple whose relationship appears healthy. Those couples that share a belief in a similar God have worked to keep him in the center of their union. The healthiest relationships will do all three.

Prayer:

God, help me to remember that I am not you.

God as We Understand Him

God as We Do Not Understand Him

Challenge:

Most of us know the frustration of repeatedly retaking our will back from our Higher Power only to find ourselves on our knees soon after and filled with despair. It is common to see that "tug-of-war" played out in romantic relationships for many years before a couple will recognize that a God is missing from their union. It was once quipped that all is fair in love and war, but if the principles of spiritual living are not applied in a romance, then love will become war.

Reflection:

If we are going to learn how to do the "next right thing" in our romantic relationship, we will need to place a God in the center of our relationship. If we are confused about how to develop a relationship with a power greater than ourselves, there are many resources available to provide guidance. If we have come to believe that a power greater than ourselves "could restore us to sanity," it is time to bring that "power" into our romances.

Prayer:

God, help me see ways of being of service to you in my romance.

God as We Understand Him

A Common Understanding

Challenge:

If you have developed a comfortable understanding of a Higher Power and learned how to draw on that power in all of your affairs, you have grown to the point that you can share it with others. You share with your fellows the things that you have to be grateful for and the ways in which your God is revealing himself to you. You have developed a habit of praying for the knowledge of God's will for you and you are looking for ways to implement that will in your life through the power he provides. You have learned that your fellowship with others in recovery is vital to your spiritual progress, but what of your relationship with your partner?

Reflection:

It is not necessary that you and your romantic partner share the same understanding of spirituality or that you have the same conception of God. What is important is that each of you spends time relating your spiritual journey with your partner. When both of you regularly participate in the practice of united prayer and meditation time, your relationship will develop a special bond. The two of you may have similar interests or hobbies that united you, but no shared activity can produce the results that common prayer and meditation time bring into being. When you both look to better understand each other's relationship with a Higher Power, then spirituality will assume a bigger place in your relationship.

Prayer:

God, help me to seize opportunities to share my experience of you with my romantic partner. I know that you have given us this gift of romantic love and that you long to enrich it for us.

God as We Understand Him

Behaving as God Would

Challenge:

We are invited by our God to "love one another" as he has loved us. Unfortunately, it is quite demanding to practice our spiritual love in all of our affairs. It can be especially difficult to behave as a Higher Power would have us behave in our romantic relationships. We tend to place a great many expectations on a romantic relationship. We expect to always feel wanted and appreciated. We expect to feel special and supported in all that we do. When these expectations are not met, we can become lost in feelings of entitlement and rejection. We become demanding and even attacking when we believe that our partner has slighted us. We are sure that we are right and certain that our partner is wrong. Our actions can begin to suffocate the relationship.

Reflection:

It is understandable to turn to a romantic partner when we are in emotional need, but sometimes the other person is in as great a need as we are even though the need is not openly expressed. What do we do with the real feelings of rejection and hurt? If your partner's response to your need is not satisfying you, reach out to others who are perhaps more spiritually fit. If your partner seems to be afraid to answer your knock on the door, let him/her know you are available when they are ready.

Prayer:

God, help me to be direct in the expression of my needs and desires without being demanding. Please teach me to respond to the messengers that you send me. I know that I cannot always get love from the places that I desire.

God as We Understand Him

When Your Partner Needs a Light

Challenge:

There are few times in a romance that are more frightening then when both of partners are lost in the darkness of depressions or the maniacal whirling of their respective defects of character. The crisis can be further complicated by a faulty perception that it is really our partner and not us that is in trouble. It may be that you do not see the danger you are in because your concern for your partner is so great. Whatever the reason for your concern and regardless of whether or not you can see your part, you must act. But where do we begin?

Reflection:

If you believe the spiritual axiom that states "whenever we are disturbed, no matter what the cause, there is something wrong with us," you must assume that your mate is not the only one in the dark. Rather than begin with your mate, look at yourself. Examine your thoughts, feelings, and behaviors to determine what defect in your character is causing you to deal with your feelings in such an unproductive manner. Get honest with a friend or sponsor about the feelings and motivations that you are experiencing in order to get input on what behaviors you might begin to change. As you change your behaviors toward your partner, your feelings for and toward them will change and you will find yourself in a position to be of help. When your partner needs to see the light, cast it first on yourself.

Prayer:

God, help me to see you clearly so I can better know myself.

God as We Understand Him

Weekend Workshop

Our decision to bring the God of our understanding into the center of our relationship came at a time of shared desperation. We found ourselves running constantly from each other and were frightened that our relationship would not survive to see our first wedding anniversary. We have celebrated thirty-three anniversaries since then and the power we have derived from our faith in our God has forged a romantic and spiritual union beyond our wildest imaginations. We pray that you will find the power you need to love each other as your God would have it.

John & Elaine

My Gifts to the Partnership

Describe, in writing, a time during the past year that you needed direction or support and you failed to ask for your partner's help.

Describe, in writing, a time during the past year when you believed that your partner needed your direction or support and you failed to make your insights known to him/her.

Share with your partner your perception of what your God has done for the relationship.

We Had a Spiritual Awakening

As a Result of These Steps...

Challenge:

The 12th Step of *Alcoholics Anonymous* (1953, p. 60) reads, "Having had a spiritual awakening as a result of these steps, we tried to carry this message to alcoholics, and to practice these principles in all our affairs." The 12th Step introduces you to the promise of a spiritual awakening if the preceding steps are followed, and suggests that this promise will be sustained by taking the actions of trying to help others and practice the 12 Steps in all of your affairs. If your romantic relationship is feeling "dry" and lacking richness, it may be that you and/or your partner have failed to apply each of the first 11 Steps to your relationship. It is common for romantic partners to have done a great deal of work on themselves individually that they have not applied to their romance. If the partners fail to do so, the relationship will be deprived of a spiritual awakening.

Reflection:

The practice of incorporating your personal Step work into your romantic relationship is vital to the relationship's longevity. Shared 3rd Step time will enhance your focus on a power greater than the relationship. Exposing elements of your respective 4th Steps will provide your partner with the information they will need to respond empathically to your needs. Relating the knowledge that you have about your defects of character may allow your partner to assist you in the development of a plan for bringing those shortcomings to your God in the 7th Step. The regular practice of shared prayer and meditation will strengthen the spiritual foundation of your union. You can have dry or rich and warm – which is it?

Prayer:

God, help me to practice all 12 of the Steps in my romance so that we may enjoy the spiritual awakening you have promised.

We Had a Spiritual Awakening

Feelings Wake Up Grumpy

Challenge:

Prior to having a spiritual awakening, you can expect that an emotional awakening will be necessary and eventual. The feelings that awaken during the development or enhancement of a romantic relationship will generally wake up grumpy. If your relationship is only now beginning to emerge from active dependency, then the grumpy feelings that arise will be related to the injuries that the two of you have endured during the dependency's progression. If your relationship is in its infancy, it is not likely to have many memories of its own. However, that does not mean there will be no emotional discomfort. Just the contrary; every new romance will eventually awaken the memories of previous romantic relationships. If those relationships were painful, then the feelings associated with those memories will be grumpy. So, be on your toes and prepare for a grump!

Reflection:

Oftentimes, grumpy feelings scare the respective members of a romance, regardless of what stage of development that the relationship is in. If it is a new relationship, the grumpy feelings may leave the partners fearful that the relationship is doomed because the "sparkle" is gone so quickly. If the relationship is crawling out from beneath the rubble of a ruinous dependency, then the grumpy feelings may leave the members less hopeful that the romantic sparkle of the past can be re-ignited. Whatever the basis for the fear, you need not be too alarmed. These feelings are likely. If you work through the discomfort without pushing each other away, the pain will dissipate and the sparkle will remind you of the Fourth of July fireworks of your youth.

Prayer:

God, help me to remember that my grumpy feelings point to unfinished emotional or spiritual business that I must attend to. Help me to not run before I get a chance to see the sparkle.

We Had a Spiritual Awakening

Minds Wake Up Groggy

Challenge:

When a spiritual awakening occurs in a relationship, the fog begins to clear and the couple is able to see more clearly how to bring the knowledge of their God's will for them into practice. Before the fog clears and the emotional awakening is fully developed, the confusion they experience can be disabling. One or both of the partners is likely to misinterpret the other's communication and attribute motives to behavior that are inaccurate. Each is likely to think that their own form of communication is clear and concise and do not understand why their partner does not get it. They suspect that their partner understands exactly what is being said, but is choosing to hide behind game-playing tactics. The more "right" that each partner becomes, the greater the division is in their romance. A spiritual awakening will be delayed by this division. If you want the fog to lift, you must take a greater sense of responsibility for the quality of your life.

Reflection:

The feelings that you are having are real, but they are yours. Your partner has not given them to you. Nobody can make you feel anything. I know what you're thinking: I let him/her push my buttons and make me feel bad – nope wrong again! Nobody can make you feel anything. Your feelings are your responsibility, even though you may not have been able to do anything to prevent the situation in which the feelings were born. That is not to say that we are responsible for all of our pain. We did not cause it all, but we must take responsibility for it all or it will not lessen and the fog will not clear. If we want to clear away the emotional wreckage of our past we must first take responsibility for the "clean-up" rather than focusing our energies on identifying the cause.

Prayer:

God, guide me through the grogginess of my emotional awakening so that I may be able to see clearly the feelings that I am experiencing and develop strategies for coping other than blaming other people for them.

We Had a Spiritual Awakening

Spirits Wake Up Refreshed

Challenge:

The spiritual awakening you have been promised is real. At the same time, if it is your first, it may be a bit overwhelming. For some of you, the awakening of your spirit will be frightening because you will be experiencing emotions and developing insights that you have never known before. When the emotional fog begins to clear, you will begin to feel peaceful and find rest in the certain knowledge that you are being cared for. While it is nice, the calm you begin to experience may not necessarily produce the happiness you have sought in the time frame you have designed. That happiness is directly connected to your acceptance of your Higher Power's will for you. If it is happiness you are looking for, you may be disappointed with your spiritual awakening. Please do not lose focus, as you have not been cheated. It will come as you continue to practice these principles in all of your affairs, especially your romance.

Reflection:

One of the direct outcomes of the spiritual awakening that you have been promised is a fresh outlook on life and a clear vision of how your God would have you serve him in your romance. The changes in your outlook will seem gradual to you, but others, especially your romantic partner, will find them quite remarkable. As your partner responds receptively to your changed outlook, you will find yourself more inspired to continue on the path that you have begun and your changes will become more noticeable to you. The primary purpose of the spiritual awakening that awaits you is the enhancement of your ability to be of service to your God, so do not be surprised as you lose interest in yourself and gain interest in your partner.

Prayer:

God, prepare me to accept the bounty of gifts that you have prepared for me. Give me opportunities to use those gifts in service to you in my romance.

We Had a Spiritual Awakening

In All of Our Affairs

Challenge:

The awakening that you are experiencing in your romantic life will become wondrous indeed. However, the fireworks cannot be contained within the confines of the romance. We must, if we desire a lasting awakening, be prepared to practice the spiritual principles of recovery in all of our affairs. Simply put, this means that we must treat all we meet with the same dignity and respect that we extend to our romantic partner. We must maintain one and only one set of rules for living. We cannot cheat others without becoming dishonest with our mate. We cannot disregard others without discrediting the value of our mate. We cannot treat ourselves to seemingly harmless flirtations without undermining the value of our mate. There can be only one you!

Reflection:

The awakening of your spirit produces a sense of freedom and paves the way for a lasting happiness. It also includes an obligation that you commit yourself to the practice of "one" you. You cannot have a set of rules for how to behave when you are working that are different from the rules for romantic engagement. The decision to be one in the spirit of a loving God requires that you are willing to be "one." Every decision that you make in dealing with others will have an eventual impact on your romantic relationship because your behavior creates changes in your personality. We bring our personalities to all of our relationships. The same is true for the obligation you have to treat your romance with the same empathy and understanding you would a needy friend. At the same time, if you mistreat your partner, you will eventually mistreat those around you and yourself.

Prayer:

God, help me to be "one" in the spirit and in all that I say and do.

We Had a Spiritual Awakening

Weekend Workshop

Our spiritual awakening occurred during the end of our third year together, when we faced our major heart surgery for our year-old, first-born child. The individual desperation we endured that year was unsurpassed by any historical trauma, and there had been plenty. We discovered that when we allowed a God to work through us, our union acquired a strength that neither of us had been able to find on our own. Call on your God to have his power flow through your union.

John & Elaine

My Gifts to the Partnership

Write a sentence or two about each time you can recall being able to rely on a power greater than yourself.

Write a prayer of thanksgiving to your God for the power that you have been able to draw on.

Share the prayer you wrote above with your partner.

Ask your partner to share with you a time when he/she drew on his/her God's power.

Romantic Health

Gifts

Challenge:

Self-examination is an activity that becomes easier with practice. In the early stages of recovery, many of us found it difficult to perform a thorough self-examination of our emotional and spiritual health without the aid of our sponsor or spiritual advisor. While such support is invaluable, it is not always available.

Reflection:

When outside help is not readily available, there are a number of tools you can use to examine your romantic health. A spot-check inventory of the types of gifts you have chosen for your mate during the past year will provide you with a useful snapshot. Have all your gifts been practical? When you were preparing the gifts, were you excited? When your partner received the gift did he/she seem to feel appreciated? Have your gifts to your partner brought you lasting pleasure?

Prayer:

God, help me to choose gifts for my partner that enhance our romantic pleasure.

Romantic Health

Celebrating Chores

Challenge:

A romantic relationship can grow stale when the drudgery of life's chores becomes the focus of your lives together. It can seem like there is no time to relax or enjoy each other's company. Many couples choose to divide the work in an effort to move through the "to do" list faster. While this strategy can be effective with certain tasks, there will be far too many opportunities to be apart from each other.

Reflection:

When planning your chores look for opportunities to work together rather than for ways to split tasks to save time. If splitting up the chores is creating less together time, consider doing many of the "jobs" together. Errands can be run as a relay race that has predetermined rendezvous points to catch up with each other. Maintenance tasks can be split into two roles that work together (one cuts the grass while the other weeds the flower beds). It may seem like you are getting less done, but you will have more fun doing it. You will also be creating memories that will comfort you during the times when you are not able to connect with each other.

Prayer:

God, help me to think of "us," rather than splitting up tasks.

Romantic Health

Spontaneity

Challenge:
Much of our lives are scheduled. A job demands that we be in a certain place at a certain time. The children have activities galore. There is church and meetings and chores, and traffic. When will we ever find time to be spontaneous with all that we are obligated to do? Some of us cannot remember when we had a spontaneous romantic thought that did not involve sex. While there is a great deal to be said for the adventure of spontaneous sexual activity, we are suggesting that you look, in general, at spontaneity in your relationship.

Reflection:
When you think of your partner, a spontaneous prayer of gratitude is a marvelous gift. A phone call or email during the course of the day is a delightful way of communicating the interest that your partner holds in your busy day. Meet your partner for lunch or dinner on the run. Plan a short vacation that you surprise your unsuspecting partner with. It will be romantic to plan for and it will be romantic to be surprised with for your partner. If necessary, plan time to allow for you to be spontaneous. That sounds crazy, but it may be that your lack of romantic spontaneity is related to the pressure you feel to perform. Set aside time to think romantically and you will begin to think more romantically.

Prayer:
God, help me to slow down long enough to be excited about my romantic love.

Romantic Health

Gratitude

Challenge:

When our relationship is experiencing poor romantic health, we are not likely to view each other as valuable. Our tendency during times of "soul sickness" is to see the flaws in our partner's character. Our partner's behavior will become increasingly less tolerable and our attention will be drawn to the ways in which it seems that our partner detracts from the quality of our life. To make matters worse, it is common for both partners in a romantic relationship to wander into the same abyss during the same period of illness. When that happens, it is unlikely that either person will be able to see the ways in which they are contributing to the disease. Each will be able to see the other partner's faults with crystal clarity. This fog will sometimes lift on its own but, in most cases, one or both partners will have to care enough to step outside the relationship for help.

Reflection:

When all you can see is your partner's shortcomings it will become difficult to invest understanding and support into your relationship. As your investment lessens you will derive less and less joy from the spirit-centered act of bringing love to others. If the condition persists, your whole outlook on life will begin to deteriorate as your emotional and spiritual insecurity grows. When you want to fault-find, stop! Look at your partner and all that you have been through together and build a gratitude list of all that he/she represents in your life. Your outlook upon life and your partner will change. The change will allow you to provide the support that he/she may need to get unstuck.

Prayer:

God, help me to be grateful for what I have, as it will help me live in the now with you instead of the future or the past without you.

Romantic Health

Focused Prayer

Challenge:

During difficult times in a romantic relationship, the fear and insecurity at the basis of unhappiness is likely to drain any spiritual reserves you have accumulated. Generally, if you examine your practices of prayer and meditation during romantic ill-health, you will find that you have gotten very sloppy. When your attention is alarmed by the growing absence of thoughtful prayer, it is normal to begin frantic prayers for healing about the things we have identified as being wrong with the relationship. We pray for communication, honesty, openness, and, most of all, for our partner to change. Oops—how did that get in there? Yes, many of us will find ourselves focusing our prayers on what we would like our partner to do for us or themselves rather than what we can do.

Reflection:

When you find yourself in romantic ill health, pray for healing of the romance. Pray to be reintroduced to the excitement you once found in mutual discovery and self-disclosure. Pray for the return of sexual excitement and passionate thoughts. Pray for the return of the spirit of love that once dwelt in your romance. Praying for romance is romantic, so you are on your way.

Prayer:

God, help me to love as you love, with excitement, passion, and healing.

Romantic Health

Weekend Workshop

The maintenance of a healthy romantic life, as we discovered, was every bit as important as our physical well-being or economic security. Your approach can either be reactive or proactive. You can go either way; until you are suffering the pains of a failing romance or plan romantic events before you need them. Your romantic life is like a buffet table: filled with culinary delights. You can decide on just a ham sandwich if you want. It took us a while but we eventually decided that we wanted it all. We hope you do not settle for the sandwich.

John & Elaine

My Gifts to the Partnership

Write a paragraph or two of all the times you settled for romantic "ham sandwiches" and share it with a member of your support group.

Ask your God to reveal to you what is possible in a sober, healthy romance.

Share with your partner one item you would like to include in your romantic life that is not physically sexual.

A Member of My Support Group

Who Knows Me Better

Challenge:

Romantic couples are often encouraged by their sponsors or other well-meaning members of their fellowship to maintain separate programs of recovery. While it makes good sense for each member of the relationship to take full responsibility for the quality of his or her own respective recovery, it does not make sense to isolate your partner from your recovery program. In relationships where the partners share all of the most intimate life details with their support group members to the exclusion of their mate, those relationships often experience severe communication and emotional intimacy problems. A division develops or widens between the romantic partners who do not confide in each other or fail to accept meaningful input from each other. There can be no future without trust.

Reflection:

It is important to develop sources of support outside of the romantic relationship because it can be difficult at times to get objective input from a loved one. However, you will be deprived of potentially valuable insights if you do not incorporate your mate into your support group. As most of us have already discovered, it is much easier to be "sober" at our 12 Step meetings than it is at home. Part of the reason is because the members of our household have the opportunity to view all of our moods and are likely to know us at our spiritual worst. Another reason that is perhaps less obvious is that we are likely to be more open to input when we are with members of our support group. If you are willing to take the risk to involve your mate in your recovery, you will be grateful for the richness that develops in your relationship.

Prayer:

God, help me to see you in all the people in my life, not just those I am comfortable exposing myself to. I need to learn from everyone and I routinely fall into disrepair when I shun the "teachers" I will be taught by.

A Member of My Support Group

You Are Either a Student or a Teacher

Challenge:

A once popular, but now obscure recovery slogan cautioned that there are only two types of alcoholics: students and teachers. The teachers relapse and the students observe and remain sober. The warning discouraged the sufficient deacons of recovery from failing to learn from each and every person they encountered. The cautious recovery members were encouraged to practice rigorous self-examination and observe closely the differences between those who relapsed and those whose lives became fuller. You can remain "sober" as long as you remain a student. You will be a successful student when you do not choose who your teachers are going to be.

Reflection:

There is much for us to learn about ourselves in recovery and the journey can be made much less painful if we remain open to those who know us. The fears that we experience in a romantic relationship often awaken defects in our character that are not evident in other situations or relationships in our lives. Your romantic partner will have the opportunity to see you in situations that your recovery friends will not. If you allow your mate to be a mirror in which to examine your behavior and motives, you will develop a fuller understanding of your defects of character. This unparalleled insight will enhance the depth and scope of the interventions that you will be able to impose on your defects of character. You can be injured by what you do not see. You can be brought to healing by allowing your mate to be your "eyes."

Prayer:

God, help me to see with the eyes of those I love and those who chose to love me. Relieve me of the blindness that comes with self-sufficiency and defensiveness.

A Member of My Support Group

Teaching Others to Care for Us

Challenge:

The people we have drawn into our personal support group have gained access because we have trusted them with our innermost selves. Trust, we are certain, has taken time and cannot be easily replicated. We believe that these special people have gained our trust through the quality of their responsiveness to the material we have shared with them over the months and years. Oftentimes, we judge our support group members to be more trustworthy than our romantic partners because they have been there without resentment or judgment when we have needed them. Perhaps they have received us without criticism because they were not a part of our riotous past and are not exposed to the day-to-day changes in our moods. They have generally found us open and receptive to their offers of help. Our romantic partners, on the other hand, may have been blocked many times when they extended themselves to us.

Reflection:

A romantic relationship can become a trustworthy source of support if we are willing to teach our mates how we prefer to be cared for. We need to show them where we hurt and help them to understand how it feels. We need to avoid making unrealistic demands on them to fix the parts of us that are broken. We need to make amends to them for the ways that they have been hurt by us in order to expect that they would be able to respond to us without resentment or skepticism. When we have an emotional need we want them to address, we must tell them what we are looking for rather than to leave them to guess on their own. Finally, we must teach them by the example that we show them when they are in need of our support.

Prayer:

God, help me to be an example of unbiased love and support to my mate in all that I do.

A Member of My Support Group

Taking Responsibility

Challenge:

If you are going to accept the responsibility for supporting your mate in his/her recovery efforts, there are a few potential obstacles that you should examine. First, do not give your mate input without their informed consent. Second, be prepared to expose yourself at great depths because it is your experience, strength, and hope that will most benefit your mate. Lastly, you must be willing to let go of the outcome of the support that you offer.

Reflection:

If you agree to join your mate's support group, you will have an obligation to serve as a mirror for him/her to examine him/her selves in. The input that you have to offer is only valuable if it is desired. You can not help someone against their will, so make sure that your partner understands what the input that they are consenting to is all about. Do not begin with, "Can I tell you something?" because they may not be ready for the subject. Tell them what you want to talk about. You can only help another with material that you can identify with so it is dangerous to move beyond your experience, strength, and hope. Finally, the help that you are offering needs to come without hitches. If your partner gets uncomfortable and starts shutting down, you need to assume that you no longer have permission to share. Likewise, if your partner accepts that input and chooses not to act on it, then you must leave the outcome to a Higher Power.

Prayer:

God, help me to share all that I have with my mate in a style that you would approve of. Let my words be loving and nonjudgmental. Let my actions be caring and purposeful. Let my prayers for healing be never-ending.

A Member of My Support Group

God as Our Sponsor

Challenge:

A decision to invite your mate into your support group can seem like the ultimate risk of self-exposure, but it is not nearly as scary as deciding that you will be a part of his/her support group. If your mate is an active part of your support group, you will no longer be able to behave differently at home than you do at a meeting. The decision to invite him/her in that close can be risky because there will be certain favorite defects of character that you will have to be prepared to have removed. Likewise, making a decision to actively support your partner's recovery efforts will necessitate a change in your rules of engagement. Many times, we can convince our support group members that our romantic partners are the root of our emotional unhappiness. If you are supporting your mate's recovery it will become very difficult to make him/her the object of your blame. You cannot be on the lookout for his/her well-being and also justify blaming him/her for your emotional or spiritual distress.

Reflection:

If you and your partner have chosen to be intimate support group members for each other, it will be crucial to the relationship that you have a "Higher Power" or a God to watch over it. The concept of having a God as your relationship's sponsor may seem odd at first, but the idea will grow on you with time. The formula is easy to practice and difficult to remember when you feel the urge to run the show. If the two of you promote God as your relationship's sponsor, all that you do and plan must be brought before him for review and counsel. But how, you ask, does that work in reality? Easy, each of you should assume that you are full partners and each have 49.5% of the voting stock and that your God has the deciding 1%. If the two of you do not agree to bring the vote to God in prayer, then he will reveal his vote to the two of you during meditation time.

Prayer:

God, help me to look to you when I am confused about how to be a full partner in my romance.

A Member of My Support Group

When we began hitting emotional obstacles as our relationships developed, we got a great deal of unsolicited advice from our fellow sufferers. Most of the advice supported our own prideful idea that the problem was the other person. The other really plentiful input focused on our need to lead separate, seemingly unconnected programs of recovery. These two examples of advice helped us to understand the reason for the suggestion that: "you should not ask for advice because you might get it; you should not give it because somebody might take it." We were naïve enough to ask for it but, thankfully, we were sober enough to not follow it. We learned to seek out those people who, by their example, showed us how to support each other. We did not need to disconnect from each other. We needed to take responsibility for our own individual recoveries. We hope you will consider inviting your partner into a more intimate place in your support group.

John & Elaine

My Gifts to the Partnership

Examine whether or not you have done something to promote the perception held by others that your partner is your problem.

Make a concerted effort to clear up that confusion with each person who has that feeling.

Ask your partner for ways that you could be more supportive in his/her recovery.

Pick at least one strategy to begin working on.

Thanksgiving

Counting Our Blessings

Challenge:

There are a great many challenges to the security of a romantic relationship. The fears of our past life experiences may threaten the safety that we feel with each other. The demands that are placed on our available time sometimes make it difficult for us to commit either quality or quantity time to our union which would promote mutual security. The projections we have regarding our ability to handle the economic vulnerabilities of career or childrearing obligations that await us can seem overwhelming at times. Sometimes, this and other challenges will leave you or your partner unsure of the value of your romantic union. This and other questions can create a wall between your relationship and the God of your understanding that will cast a shadow on your faith. Any shadow that blocks out your God's warmth will leave the relationship cold and dry.

Reflection:

Your union, if it is of God, has great value to you and others. If either of you have begun to question the benefit of your union, take some time to examine the contributions your relationship has made to your lives and the lives of those you have touched. Perhaps your communication or honesty need some fine-tuning, but a "dry" period does not have to create a division. Look closely at the blessings that both of you have received as a result of trying to serve your God. Examine carefully the gifts that your union has given to those who have been close to you. If a state of gratitude is difficult to obtain on your own, ask your partner what he/she is grateful for and you will be inspired.

Prayer:

God, help me to see the blessings that I/we have received. Show me where to share your gifts with others so that my void will be filled and others will know your love.

Thanksgiving

Expressing Thanks

Challenge:

We have spoken a great deal about the importance of sharing your innermost needs and experiences with your romantic partner, as it fosters a depth of trust many us have been deprived of. It is equally important, however, to regularly share your gratitude for your partner directly to him/her. It is easy to take for granted that our partner, who knows our secrets, must know how grateful we are for what he/she has brought to our life. We are confident that the times of deep sharing have contained the kind of dialogue that would sufficiently communicate to our partner how important he/she is to us. Why, we ask, must we remind our partner of his/her importance to us? He/she must certainly know by now!

Reflection:

Sharing our thanksgiving with our partner is much more than saying "thank you" to him/her. When you take the time to prepare a list of those qualities in your partner that you are particularly grateful for, you will be affirming the risks your partner has taken to fully commit himself/herself to the relationship. If you support the list with specific examples of when you benefited from each of those qualities, you will provide your partner with a clear picture of the way in which a Higher Power is working through him/her to touch the lives of others. This confirmation of being a spiritual vessel in service to others will provide your partner with the basis for personal gratitude at times when he/she is feeling low. Thanksgiving is a gift that keeps on giving.

Prayer:

God, help me to remember to praise your work that is provided through the efforts of those that love me.

Thanksgiving

Acting Grateful

Challenge:
Every generation has known periods of fear and pessimism. Our time is no different than the other periods in history when people feared for their economic security and personal safety. Every day, broadcast news and print media focus our attention on what is wrong in the world and enhance our sense of vulnerability. It is good to be informed about the world we live in, but there will be times when the plethora of shock and awe that we are exposed to leaves us feeling impotent and focused on what we are missing, and not on what we have.

Reflection:
A state of gratitude generates a calming sense of security as it promotes a feeling of fulfillment. A decision to behave as a person with gratitude requires that you take positive assertive action toward the development of security for others. You have a great deal to be grateful for in your love relationship that, when shared with others, can serve as a taproot for them to develop hope. Behave as a person of gratitude. Refuse to listen to or participate in gossip. Ignore opportunities to relate sensational news stories to others who will be emotionally burdened by them. Highlight the positive qualities in the lives of the people that you know. Let those who are struggling know you care through your sacrifice of time and talent. Bring your relationships to those who have none in a way that gives them hope for their future. Behaving in a way that displays gratitude leaves you feeling more grateful.

Prayer:
God, help me to show others all that I am grateful for. Let them be inspired by my faith, nurtured by my kindness, and feel grateful for my support.

Thanksgiving

Worry or Pray

Challenge:

Life sometimes seems like a long string of unanswered questions. When we are uncertain and fearful about the outcome of an important event, whether it is related to health, finances, romance or some other critical area of our life situation, we tend to feel like there is something that we should do. We are frequently completely powerless over a particular outcome or the time it takes to receive the news. We can push, prod, argue, and demand but we are, in reality, in control of very little other than our own behavior. How we behave when we are fearful or anxious about some unknown will affect our body, mind, and spirit. Many of us learned, by example, to worry when we were uncertain or fearful. The act of worrying was presented to us as if it were an actual "something" that we could do about a situation over which we had no real control. Some of us even learned that a person worried about another person because they loved that person. That made for a very confusing mess for the unspoken implication was: "if you do not worry then you must not love."

Reflection:

The practice of worrying is learned, and anything that is learned can be unlearned. The unlearning can begin with the use of a simple phrase: if you pray, why worry and if you worry, why pray? Worrying is what we do when we are not talking about our feelings to those we love. If we talk about our feelings to those we love in the company of our God, we are praying. Let us be grateful for the opportunity to learn new skills and discard broken ones.

Prayer:

God, help me to share honestly with those I love all that I think and feel. Teach me how to reach out and practice powerlessness.

Thanksgiving

Helping Others Find the Way

Challenge:

Gratitude is not an emotional state that we can be made to feel even though some members of the "sobriety police force" believe that they are in charge of enforcing the law. It is not uncommon to hear that someone who was feeling emotionally stuck in his/her recovery was accosted by a fellowship member and beat with the "gratitude stick" because they were complaining and should have been grateful. Whether or not the sufferer had reason to be grateful or not is really beside the point. When we are distraught, it is not comforting to be shamed by a recovery peer into covering up the distress and pretending to be grateful. Those who choose to impose gratitude on others would appear to be acting on their own behalf. If your partner's emotional or spiritual condition is causing you distress, get help for yourself before you try to help your partner. If you encounter a lack of gratitude in others, make a decision to show them the way rather than beat them up.

Reflection:

The way to gratitude is faith. Faith would appear to be a product of having gone through difficult times with the help of my God and my fellows. Moving through pain or distress with the help of those who love me teaches me to rely on a power outside of myself. I may not think that I can handle it, but I come to trust that I can. When you encounter distress in those you care for, meet them where they are, share your experience and faith, and you will give rise to gratitude.

Prayer:

God, help me to show others my gratitude through my willingness to be of service to them during their times of need.

Thanksgiving

There are times of the year when we have either found ourselves feeling blessed or cursed. If you are struggling to identify sources of gratitude in your life, our hearts go out to you. We have found ourselves more than once confused and wandering through a spiritual desert. If you are lost, look skyward rather than at the ground and acknowledge your willingness before your Higher Power. If you find your supply of gratitude brimming over, rejoice and share it with others.

John & Elaine

My Gifts to the Partnership

Retreat to a quiet place and prepare a gratitude list that you can update every year to mark your progress.

Perform an act of gratitude in secrecy.

Prepare a list of what you are grateful for in your romantic relationship and share it with your partner.

We Knew We Were Somewhat at Fault...

We Knew We Were Somewhat at Fault...

Challenge:

It is difficult when we are feeling hurt and fearful to examine the situation or the relationship with a focus on our own faults. It is so much easier to see where our partner has been unkind, judgmental, or unresponsive. We see the faults of those we love with clarity. Our perception of our mate's current behavior is magnified by his/her past behaviors. We can see that he/she is "really to blame because this is exactly what he/she has done before!" At the moment of our injury, the past and the present become one and intensify each other like looking through a magnifying glass. We use the past as proof that what we are interpreting is accurate and just. Even though we might be certain that the other person is more to blame than we are, we must look at our own wrongs.

Reflection:

If we repeatedly fail to examine our own wrongs in our romantic relationship, the intimacy that we have developed will begin to drain off. The intimate bond our relationship relies on is a mutual trust and that trust can not be sustained if we are always blaming our mate or always assuming all the responsibility for the problems we are experiencing. We generally get a glimpse that we may be somewhat at fault, and that should be our only focus until we have completely cleaned our side of the street. When we have taken our wrongs through Steps 6, 7, and 8 and made a full amends, then, and only then, can we be sure the problem that remains is our mate's.

Prayer:

God, help me to look first at myself. I need to see where I have been wrong and how that wrong is perpetuated by my thinking and strategies for coping with my feelings.

We Knew We Were Somewhat at Fault…

Understanding Resentment

Challenge:

Our ability to see the wrongs in others, as we introduced yesterday, is largely related to the tendency of past life experiences to intensify the feelings of a present day situation. The feelings associated with an unresolved crisis in our relationship's past will amplify the feelings we experience in a present day conflict because we have not adequately addressed them. If our mate was dishonest with our finances in the past and the crisis was "resolved" by both agreeing that each of us had been guilty of overspending at times, the feelings associated with the harm we felt will not be resolved. We may have agreed to stop fighting, but the feelings are likely to linger on under the surface until the next "wrong" occurs and we erupt with seemingly "justified" anger and resentment. Resentment is a re-feeling of a past harm. If we are resentful then "it" was not really resolved.

Reflection:

Feelings are resolved when we bring the events, which precipitated them through Steps 4 through 9. When we have accepted a detailed 9th Step from our partner that includes an acknowledgement of the defects of character associated with the wrong, a plan for change, and a heartfelt request for forgiveness, the feelings associated with the injury will heal. The healing we speak of does not erase the memory of the event, but the powerful emotional surge is no longer present. Our mate could wrong us again in a similar incident and we would not react as if "nothing has changed."

Prayer:

God, help me to work on the healing of the feelings associated with the injuries that I have endured, as well as the injuries that I have perpetrated. Show me how to make amends that actually promote mending.

We Knew We Were Somewhat at Fault...

Yeah, But

Challenge:

Why is it that most of us become defensive when we are confronted with some harmful behavior of ours? When a partner suggests that we are behaving in a way that he/she finds hurtful, we quickly assume one of three positions: 1) we deny having done what we are being accused of, 2) we attempt to blame our mate or someone else for why we are behaving the way that we are, or 3) we offensively target the wrongs that our mate has perpetrated on us that have not been corrected. Why such defensiveness? What are we afraid of? How long has this seemingly automatic reaction in us been our method of dealing with "bad" news?

Reflection:

When our mate gives us feedback about how he/she feels about us and our response begins with "yeah, but," we are most likely responding with a defense that has been with us since early childhood. If you grew up in an environment in which people successfully blamed other people for the quality of their own life as a way of coping with disappointment, then you are likely to suffer with this defect of character. When we were children, the use of "yeah, but," like most defects of character, became a way of coping with the uncomfortable emotional experiences we were exposed to. The contestants in the "blame game" were going to find someone to hold responsible for the crisis and we did not want it to be us. Now as adults, we continue to respond with the defense, even when it no longer provides insulation from hurt. We are now trying to grow in the image and likeness of our Higher Power and there can be no room for defensiveness.

Prayer:

God, help me to stay open to all that I may learn about myself from the people that love me.

We Knew We Were Somewhat at Fault...

The Search Light

Challenge:

When we are attempting to examine the dynamics of a disturbing situation it can be difficult to clearly illuminate the events that occurred. Most of us tend to have better recall for how we felt rather than what we said or how we behaved. We are almost always certain about what our mate said and did even when we are extremely foggy about our own actions. If it is difficult to see the details concerning our behavior, we need more light. The light may come from our sponsor, our recovery journals, our inventories, or prayer and meditation.

Reflection:

If we have maintained an open line of communication with our sponsor, we can go to him/her and ask for input about our role in the event under scrutiny. It may be necessary to instruct your sponsor to keep the focus on you and not your partner because we have a way of steering responsibility away from ourselves. The practice of maintaining a daily feeling journal can prove to be most helpful when you are confused about your role in a given situation. Flipping through the journal in search of times when you had feelings similar to the ones you are now experiencing is likely to produce some insight into how you may have behaved in the crisis you are examining. Lastly, bring the event before a power greater than yourself in prayer and ask that he scan your behavior with his searchlight and your meditation time will illuminate your contribution to the conflict.

Prayer:

God, help me to use all the resources available to me to see through the shadows of my defensiveness. I want to change what needs to be changed, but I need help to see myself clearly.

We Knew We Were Somewhat at Fault...

We Are Responsible for the Quality of Our Own Life

Challenge:

True and lasting sobriety is predicated on the belief that we are responsible for the quality of our own lives. If we are unhappy, we hold the responsibility for that unhappiness. If we are not feeling fulfilled, we hold the responsibility for the emptiness. If we continue to relapse into our destructive obsessions, we are responsible for the decision to do so, as well as the outcome of the relapse. We may not see the truth in those statements at the time because we are prone to blame other people for making us feel bad. When our focus is on other people, places, and things it is easy to relapse "at them." "He pushed my buttons!" "She rejected me." "They did not understand and were not the least bit supportive." "Who could blame me?"

Reflection:

If you and your partner are going to enjoy a lasting, loving, sober relationship, you will each need to take full and complete responsibility for the quality of your own lives. The act of taking responsibility for the quality of your own life will include the following: taking responsibility for your behavior, taking responsibility for your feelings, and taking responsibility for the words that you use to describe them. If you or your partner relapses back into harmful dependency, it will be for only one reason – a decision to change the way you feel. The major emotional task of recovery is to find alternative methods for coping with our feelings other than resorting to harmful obsessions. Take responsibility for the quality of your own life and you will know incredible freedom from the "blame game."

Prayer:

God, help me to practice acceptance of my feelings. They are neither right nor wrong and I do not have to take action on all of them.

We Knew We Were Somewhat at Fault...

Weekend Workshop

We have each known times of great emotional pain when we were trapped in the web of fault-finding within our romance. We have discovered few behaviors more damaging to the security of our relationship than the practice of blaming each other for the poor quality of some aspect of our personal lives. It did not matter whether it was in the area of sex or finances; the decision to blame quickly eroded trust, stifled communication, and ejected a Higher Power from the center of our union. Blame is like kryptonite for the soul of a romance.

John & Elaine

My Gifts to the Partnership

Identify what your initial feeling reaction is to realizing that you are wrong. Look back in time to situations in which you have been wrong and see if there is a pattern to your feelings during those times.

Share what you discover with your sponsor, therapist or friend.

Share the patterns you identified in the above exercise with your partner.

Describe to your partner the last situation you can recall where you wanted to blame your feelings on someone and chose not to. Do not use an example involving your partner.

What of the Other Victims

We Are Not Alone

Challenge:

We are meant to be united, not alone. Oftentimes, high school sweethearts drift into a world unto themselves. The young couple spends countless hours on the phone and all of their free time together. One or both members of the relationship may be jealous of the attention that their partner pays to friends and social interests. The jealousy is either quickly resolved or it serves as the driving force for the partners to pull themselves into an exclusive relationship with each other as a way of handling the distress caused by the insecurity. When this happens, both people in the romance make themselves less available for love and support outside of the relationship. The couple's family and friends may protest the exclusivity, but the immature couple views the complaints as mere attempts to break them up and resolve to draw their web closer. The young relationship will most likely die an untimely death by graduation. What is the problem?

Reflection:

Some will argue that the outcome is a predictable stage in the development of youthful romantic maturity. Perhaps the perception of immaturity as the problem is accurate, but that is not related to the age of the partners. Many new relationships are ignited in recovery because we are excited by the fullness we experience in our relationship with other recovering friends. We want that fullness in a romantic relationship and the romantic relationships we pursue are initially very fulfilling. Unfortunately, many couples become obsessed with each other and lose sight of the sense of community fellowship that may have first attracted them. If the romance is the exclusive "property" of its members and "off limits" to the input from and fellowship with others, it will die an untimely death.

Prayer:

God, help me to keep my romance in the sunshine of our common fellowship. Help us to learn from others and to give to others. We cannot grow together alone.

What of the Other Victims

Has Our Relationship Injured Others

Challenge:

A romantic relationship represents a powerful force. The relationship can be a source of inspiration and hope for some and a source of conflict for others. If your romance has been a tumultuous one, then you should expect that those around you have been impacted by it. If there are children involved, the impact is certain. Your current romance may have begun in the aftermath of a previously troubled romance or contributed to the dissolution of that romance. Whatever the situation, it is likely that your romance has touched and is impacting the lives of others. Consider the impact that your romance has had on those around you and consider what needs to be done once you have brought the relationship through the 4th through 9th Steps.

Reflection:

We do not live or love in a vacuum. Our mutual love can enrich the lives of those who are near to us. Our open or concealed conflict can diminish those very same lives. If you and your partner determine either separately or together that others have suffered unnecessarily from your joint conflict, you can make an effort to mend those injuries and help others to recover. Please do not assume that the conflict resolution the two of you achieve together will be of much solace to those you have harmed unless you address it directly with them. Oftentimes, when a couple is examining their relationship for areas of needed healing, they forget that others very close to them, such as offspring or parents, have been deeply hurt by their turmoil. If we only treat the pilot and the copilot and ignore the passengers of the plane crash, do we have any reason to rejoice? Please pay attention to the help that your partner might need.

Prayer:

God, help me to remember that we are not alone and that we are always either a good or a bad example of how this program works.

What of the Other Victims

Marriage Without Romance

Challenge:

When you look around, it is clear that you are not alone in your desire for love and romance. Many couples struggle with issues of trust, intimacy, and communication. Your relationship will be observed by many and directly influence a good number of people. We have explored the benefits that you will derive from the disclosure of your romance to others in a general way. You will inspire some couples to take more risks in their relationship. Some couples that need the fellowship of another committed couple will feel blessed by the time that you give them. However, these groups barely scratch the surface of the numbers in need. Those in greatest need will be those that have settled into a tolerable co-existence as "married singles." You can be of the greatest service to the greatest number by reaching out to those couples who have settled for marriage without romance.

Reflection:

The divorce rate is staggering in the United States and the topic is of great concern and discussion by those who are conscious of social values and societal trends. The silent majority of marital casualties however, has avoided divorce and is quietly "engaged to be divorced." When a couple settles for the death of the romance that once bound them together, they have sadly resigned themselves to a slow progression toward the divorce of spirit, mind, and eventually body. If you have remained committed to the preservation of romance in your relationship, then you will be keenly aware of those who could benefit from your help. But how, you ask? Spend time in prayer and meditation with your mate to discover how the two of you can be of service to the silent masses.

Prayer:

God, help me to spread the romantic love you have blessed us with to others.

What of the Other Victims

Attraction Rather than Promotion

Challenge:

A committed romantic relationship has an enduring strength that can communicate hope to other couples who are dissatisfied with the quality of their relationship. It is easy to spot those relationships that are dying, because they emit feelings of a hopeless struggle to hang on, even though the partners are not sure of what they are hanging on to. Being a couple, you are apt to experience great empathy for other couples that are struggling in quicksand that is pulling them down further and further every day. The empathy you experience is part gift, but be careful of what you do with it. Not every couple who you see sinking and desperate for change are really ready to change. Many couples that you feel you can identify with in their desperation might not even be aware of it themselves. They may be used to the discomfort and numbness. If you promote yourselves to these couples, they are at best likely to recoil and at worst perceive your interest as a judgment and an unwanted intrusion. If you push, you may lose your opportunity to be of service at a later time.

Reflection:

The attraction that your relationship will generate will always depend on the honesty the two of you share and the degree to which each of you are spiritually focused. If you are strong in these areas, you will not need to sell yourselves to the couples that concern you. If you share openly what you have experienced together and the benefits you are enjoying, you will become a source of strong attraction. When you have the opportunity, ask the couple if you can share the story of your relationship's recovery. Say nothing about what they might need to do. Keep the focus on yourselves and only share when you have their permission to do so.

Prayer:

God, help us to be a beacon for others to come to your way of honesty, love, and hope.

What of the Other Victims

Maintaining Perspective

Challenge:

Your relationship is growing through your work in the Steps and the spiritual principles of openness, honesty, and integrity. The change you have grown through has created a strong bond between the two of you and become a source of attraction for other couples. The sharing work that we have recommended will provide the two of you with wondrous opportunities to serve your Higher Power and your fellows and you will receive great rewards in return. The commitment can be very fulfilling and equally draining.

Reflection:

While it is true that service returns spiritual strength, it is also true that the couples you will be working with can be troubled. The depth of trouble that they are experiencing may be beyond your experience, strength, and help. If this is the case, do not hesitate to recommend professional help. You may find yourselves becoming so enmeshed in their problems that you become angry and resentful towards them and cease to be a part of the solution. It is also important that you keep a close eye on your own relationship when working with others. It is not uncommon when working with troubled couples to begin to see your relationship as flawless. In comparison to others, yours looks great. Do not be lured into a false sense of immunity from difficulties just because the lives of others look worse.

Prayer:

God, help us to remain mindful that the strength we reflect comes from you. Help us to remember that we have a reprieve from the insanity that is contingent on the basis of our spiritual condition.

What of the Other Victims

Weekend Workshop

Our early marriage was a time of great isolation because of the needs of a medically fragile child. We bonded closer to each other and attempted to get our individual needs met in our respective 12 step fellowships. We, however, had little time that we could nurture our relationship with other couples. After a year of deprivation, we found the warm embrace of a support group who could speak to the needs of our partnership while accommodating the health needs of our ill child. We re-discovered what we had found to be true in the early days of our individual recoveries: We were not meant to be alone. We hope that you surround your partnership with the warm embrace of others.

John & Elaine

My Gifts to the Partnership

Reflect on the times that you have known personal loneliness. How far from your reach were those who could help? What blocked you? Share your findings with a member of your support group.

Share what you found in the above exercise with your partner.

Decide on a way that the two of you can extend your relationship to another couple.

`Tis the Season

Holiday Expectations

Challenge:

Each of us draws a mental picture when the phrase "holiday season" is introduced. For many, the image is a happy one filled with rich tradition and hope for renewal. Others dread the coming of the holidays because the images are dark or chaotic. Especially during the holiday season, many will attempt to produce the behavior and mood that others expect of them. Still others will be attempting to paint their own personal portrait of expectations into the minds of those they love. Whatever your experience, many couples encounter a great deal of stress in their relationships during the holidays. Many relationships have come to expect the agitation and the disagreements. It does not have to be that way.

Reflection:

There are no rules for how to behave during the holiday celebrations. You and your partner can share time-honored traditions or make up new ones. Your family may have rigid expectations of how the holidays are to be celebrated, but you do not have to be directed by the pictures that others have. Take time to discuss what the experiences of days past were like and what about them you would like to change. The emotional scrapbook you have contains many pictures that you can replace if the two of you have the mind to do so. Take the risk to celebrate one holiday with NO RULES!

Prayer:

God, help me to look beyond the storefront window for the picture that will celebrate life, love, and sobriety.

`Tis the Season

Ghosts of Seasons Past

Challenge:

For those of you who have holiday ghosts that haunt your plans for changing your emotional scrapbook, consider challenging the painful memories that attempt to leave you fearful of celebrations yet to come. "But how," you ask, "can I get out from underneath the shadow of the horrors that I have experienced?" For those with holiday ghosts who celebrate Thanksgiving it is not a time for giving thanks, it is a time for remembering what they have failed to achieve. Our holiday celebrations or religious observances sometimes fail to offer the freedom from our trials we seek. They can be commercial times of expected gift giving and resolutions that will never be kept. Some ask, "Why bother? The holidays are to be endured, not enjoyed."

Reflection:

The horrors you have known derive their power to ruin your future holidays from the pain and resentment you still feel for the experiences you have endured. For many, those holiday memories are tragic, but they need not control our present or future. Share the pain with those you love and resolve the painful memories as a way for making joyful ones. The pain in the past was real, but it will have been for nothing if we do not use it to make changes. Creating new memories requires that we embrace the past for what it was rather than keeping it hidden. We need to let it remind of us of how easily a child's dream can be broken. If we remember how fragile it is, we will take great care to make holidays special for someone else. When we take those actions to make memories for others, our own pictures are replaced.

Prayer:

God, help me to paint holiday pictures with the colors of hope, willingness, and acceptance.

`Tis the Season

Making New Memories

Challenge:
The haunting memories of our past can be powerful reminders of past failures or disappointments. When the painful memories haunt us, we tend to approach the holidays with fear and a rigid defensiveness. If we assume that we know what is going to happen and that it is not going to be pleasurable, we brace ourselves for the worst. This fear can set in motion a chain of events that resembles a self-fulfilling prophecy: we expect the worst and it comes. Joyful memories are encouraging reminders of what was and what can be. They, too, can create problems if we assume that a holiday season must replicate the joy in our memory.

Reflection:
Memories are best left as reminders of what was and what could be. Memories do not make for a good script by which to live our lives today. If we live full of fear, we will miss opportunities for peace and happiness. If we approach the season with dread, we will be creating painful future memories for those around us. Look at the past with an understanding that all things can change when you seek to serve rather than merely endure. You will be contributing to the memories you make this year.

Prayer:
God, help me to view the emotional scrapbook of my life through your eyes. Let me empathize with those who have suffered and rejoice with those that found a new freedom and a new happiness. Let me contribute warm and loving memories into the future reflections of those I love.

`Tis the Season

Living with Gratitude

Challenge:

It can be difficult to imagine living gratefully for all that has occurred in our lives. That would imply that some of us would need to be grateful for spoiled birthday parties, acts of incestuous abuse, battered limbs, and broken promises. These life experiences, in and of themselves, do not engender feelings of gratitude. These experiences often leave emotional and spiritual wounds that seem to never heal. So what is there to be grateful for? The holiday season can be a reminder of all that we have to feel bad about. If you choose to close yourself off from the opportunities for healing that await you, you will never rejoice and the holiday season will continue to be a series of events for you to endure.

Reflection:

You and your mate can change how you live a holiday season. While it is foolish to imagine being grateful for the abuse we endured, it is possible to get to a point where your life experiences can be of value to those who are still suffering, still enduring. It is easy to fall into the emotional trap of believing that we are defined by the way that other people treated us. We are not "damaged goods"; we are goods that were damaged and can be repaired. You can be a victim or a survivor, the choice is yours. No matter your choice, the path is not easy. Look this season to share your story with someone that will feel less soiled by knowing that you are recovering. Be grateful for the opportunities your injuries give you to be of service to others and you will be living grateful.

Prayer:

God, help me to understand that I am more than a mere product of how others treated me. I am loved and I will take that love to others. I am not "damaged goods" – I am being recycled.

`Tis the Season

Spreading the Joy

Challenge:

It can be difficult to sort through the memories of the past or restrain ourselves from unrealistic expectations for the future, but it is vital that we maintain perspective during the holidays. Perhaps more than other times of the year, our feelings are running high and our coping strategies are being stretched to the max. We should not simply hold our breath and get through it. If we do, we will survive as we usually do. If we hunker down and brace ourselves for the season of joy, we will miss out on the joy. We can cast a shadow onto the lives of those we love or spread some joy, the choice is our own.

Reflection:

We are not suggesting that you pretend to be happy while you go caroling through the streets of your neighborhood. There are countless ways of bringing joy to others during the holiday season. You can offer your time and talents in a wide variety of ways. You can take on the chores others have neglected or do not have the energy or time to perform. You can prepare thoughtful, yet inexpensive gifts that communicate that others are special. You can spread good news about those you know that is a joyful twist on gossiping. You can love someone for who they are rather than trying to manipulate them into who you want them to be. The decision to spread joy will increase your own sense of joy and fulfillment. You do not have to allow the past to control you, but know that it will not withdraw quietly, you must act. Spread the joy.

Prayer:

God, help me to see the unmet needs in others as opportunities to redefine who I am.

`Tis the Season

Weekend Workshop

Happy holidays to you and your loved ones. Regardless of one's religious or spiritual orientation, it is difficult to miss the change in mood of those we encounter during a holiday season. For some, the focus is on tasks and for others, in abundance. Whatever your situation, you can use the "season" to celebrate the lives of those you love whether they are alive or deceased. We chose years ago to celebrate the lives of those closest to us with "love letters" that replaced the more traditional commercial tokens. We pray that you focus on the expression of your love rather than actions driven by a sense of obligation.

John & Elaine

My Gifts to the Partnership

Prepare an anonymous gift for someone you love that cannot be wrapped.

Work every day for a week to increase your prayer and meditation time as your gift to your Higher Power.

Create a new tradition with your partner to replace an uncomfortable memory of seasons past.

Promises We Can Keep

Resolutions

Challenge:

Our unscientific research (we are just making this part up) indicates that the average life expectancy of a solitary New Year's resolution is 7.5 days. If made with a solemn commitment to undertake it hand and hand with our mate, the expected life span of a joint resolution made on January 1st is 6 days. We have a difficult time maintaining resolutions in which it appears that we have some control. It is nearly impossible to remain committed to a resolution in which our adherence to it is dependent on the behavior of another person. In our recovery, when we resolved that were powerless over our destructive obsession/addiction and no human power could relieve it, the result was felt at once and we were set free. A resolution, whether it is made on January 1st or April 1st, is only as good as our willingness to draw on a power greater than ourselves.

Reflection:

If you have identified aspects of your life that you believe need changing, you must first ask yourself if you want to change. If you need to change and do not want to change, the commitment will not last long. If you are serious about change, examine what you have attempted in the past and why those attempts failed. When you have a clear picture of that history, bring that picture to a fellow sufferer and solicit his/her experience, strength, and hope. Share that picture with all those who care for you and ask for their prayers. If one of your sources of support is your mate that is great; however, keep the support to the practice of shared prayer and meditation in the beginning. You do not want your partner to assume the responsibility for your recovery.

Prayer:

God, help me to avoid the tendency to beat myself up with resolutions that I am not committed to. Life is influenced by pep rallies. I cannot cheer myself into change. I know that you are ready to carry me and I will let you.

313

Promises We Can Keep

A Rearview Mirror

Challenge:

It is sometimes difficult to get a clear perspective when looking at life in the rearview mirror. However difficult, it is important for us as a couple to take regular inventory of how we have been living our lives together. The practice of taking an inventory on our active romantic relationship may seem unfamiliar at first, but when taken seriously, the effort can be very rewarding. The model the two of you choose for such an inventory is quite optional. You can use 4th Step guides, daily inventory formats, or spiritual writings. A decision to look at the relationship when it appears to be doing well may be the preventative action the two of you have been overlooking.

Reflection:

A simple, yet intensely helpful method of taking the relationship's inventory is to examine a prayer such as the Prayer of St. Francis. Read through the prayer together slowly so that you can be united in the centering force which common prayer generates. The prayer presents a number of contrasting questions about the level of spiritual service the reader is practicing in his/her life. Use the questions St. Francis asks of his God to inventory how the two of you function with each other as well as the larger community you are involved in. Avoid finger pointing or justifying problems that you might identify. The two of you will be guided by the author's dialogue to the actions you will both need to take.

Prayer:

God, make us a channel of your peace and remove from us the obstacles that make it difficult to accomplish that transformation.

Promises We Can Keep

The Courage It Took

Challenge:

The courage it took most of us to commit to an intimate relationship based on honesty, openness, and spiritual service has required more faith than most of us ever thought ourselves capable of. Those of us who had prided ourselves in needing support from no one became willing to trust in our partner. Some of us who suspected that "true love" was a fairy tale made up for the young and inexperienced began to believe in the power of love and understood that there was no love other than "true love." Still others of us learned to run toward rather than away from people. We needed courage and it was there in abundance.

Reflection:

The courage we sought to risk it all for love came from our Higher Power. We were told that romantic love was for newlyweds. That, we discovered was a lie, which someone had told to himself/herself to divert his/her attention from the work that needed to be undertaken. We were told that we only got to love once and if that was lost so was our chance at romantic happiness. That also was a hoax created by those who were afraid to move through the loss and risk openness. The courage it took to overcome the fears associated with these and other lies came from a power greater than ourselves.

Prayer:

God, reveal to me your power so that I may claim it.

Promises We Can Keep

Our Unwritten Future

Challenge:

We make a great many promises that we do not keep. Some of them are not kept because they are made to impress others or to convince them that we are truly sorry and ready to change. Some promises are not kept because they are made during a time when the object of our promise is an immature or unreasonable goal. Then there are promises that are made without the confirmation that God desires that particular goal for us. When our promises are out of sync with a Higher Power's will for us, we are likely to encounter a great deal of distress.

Reflection:

When we make promises for how we will behave in the future, we must remain aware that our Higher Power's plan for us has yet to be fully revealed to us. We often fall into the misunderstanding that God's will for us today is going to be his will for us five years from now. When we make resolutions for change, it is wise to construct those resolutions after we have spent time discerning how our God would have us serve him in all of our affairs. We can not keep a promise that is out of line with our Higher Power's will for us if we first surrendered our will and our life over to his care.

Prayer:

God, help me to remember that your plan is dynamic and that I cannot always see what is coming next. I know that you will give me direction and power when I ask.

Promises We Can Keep

The Power to Create Change

Challenge:

The 11th Step of Alcoholics Anonymous encourages us to seek "... through prayer and meditation to improve our conscious contact with God as we understood Him, praying only for the knowledge of His will for us and the power to carry that out." The focus for many of us falls on the dynamics of prayer and meditation and the great benefit of maintaining a fit spiritual condition. The path is clear. We are taught to pray. We learn to meditate with increasingly longer periods of quiet. What more is there to learn from the 11th Step?

Reflection:

The decision to live a life centered on service to our God and our fellows creates a reliable spiritual foundation from which we can face the challenges as they come. Unfortunately, we fall short of the spiritual goals that we have set for ourselves in our life in general and our romantic relationship in specific. The problem could be laziness; pride, gluttony or any number of other commonly understood defects of character. But, before you launch off on a complete rewrite of your 4th Step, consider this: the power to carry out your God's will is available from him. The promise of God's power is commonly overlooked in the practice of the 11th Step. Draw upon the power that your God has promised in all of your efforts to serve him and your fellows.

Prayer:

God, help me to remember that you are a timeless source of power.

Promises We Can Keep

Weekend Workshop

Nowadays, New Year's Eve is a time to remember the accomplishments of the year that has just past. We look at its passing with fulfillment, for we have done our very best. A few years ago, the night was spent doing things we would later regret and wish we could forget. Sobriety has helped us to look honestly at what we have contributed to life. Today, our memories, both new and old, are not too painful to recall and share with others. This week's theme was intended to offer a few simple tools for evaluating your past and planning for your future. Embrace the moment.

John & Elaine

My Gifts to the Partnership

Make a list of New Year's resolutions from your life before recovery and compare them to promises that you have made and actually kept since entering your program.

Spend time with your partner dreaming out loud about the hopes that you have for the coming year.

Appendix A: The Twelve Steps

1. We admitted we were powerless over alcohol, that our lives had become unmanageable.
2. Came to believe that a Power greater than ourselves could restore us to sanity.
3. Made a decision to turn our will and our lives over to the care of God, as we understood Him.
4. Made a searching and fearless moral inventory of ourselves.
5. Admitted to God, to ourselves, and to another human being the exact nature of our wrongs.
6. Were entirely ready to have God remove all of these defects of character.
7. Humbly asked Him to remove our shortcomings.
8. Made a list of all persons we had harmed, and became willing to make amends to them all.
9. Made direct amends to such people wherever possible, except when to do so would injure them or others.
10. Continued to take personal inventory and when we were wrong, promptly admitted it.
11. Sought through prayer and meditation to improve our conscious contact with God as we understood Him, praying only for knowledge of His will for us and the power to carry that out.
12. Having had a spiritual awakening as the result of these steps, we tried to carry this message to alcoholics, and to practice these principles in all our affairs.

ᵢ*Alcoholics Anonymous* (3ʳᵈ ed.). (1953). New York, NY: A.A. World Services, Inc. (A.A.W.S.). The Twelve Steps are reprinted with permission of A.A.W.S., Inc. Permission to reprint the Twelve Steps does not mean that A.A.W.S. necessarily agrees with the views expressed herein. A.A. is a program of recovery from alcoholism <u>only</u> - use of the Twelve Steps in connection with programs and activities which are patterned after A.A., but which address other problems, or in any other non – A.A. context, does not imply otherwise. The references made by page number in this text correspond to pages in 1953 edition of *Alcoholics Anonymous* with permission of A.A.W.S. The 12 Steps have been reprinted in their entirety for your ease of reference.